Have Heart

"Steve and Sarah Berger show us how we can
find light and life beyond death's shadow by allowing God to carry
us behind the 'Why?' to the 'What are you going to do through
this circumstance?' No one ever wants to face the heartache this
family has experienced, but the Bergers help us see up-close and
personal the power of love and the beauty
of life in God's eternal presence."

JAMES ROBISON,
Founder and President, LIFE Outreach International

"Like Steve and Sarah, Nancy and I have a son in
Heaven. It wasn't until we looked at Heaven as the country that our
son now inhabits that it yielded its truths to us in an undeniable
way. This book illuminates the glorious truths about our future
home with a life-changing force and a biblical depth that makes it a
'must read' for all who have made travel plans for Heaven."

DR. CHUCK MISSLER,
Founder of Koinonia Institute

"Framed within the most intimate of losses,
this book allows its readers to peek into life-and-death
perspectives of those who follow Jesus."

WILLIAM PAUL YOUNG,
Author of New York Times Best Seller, The Shack

"The story of the life of Josiah Berger should be shared far and wide. From this most tragic accident, there came life. Josiah's decision to donate his organs allowed 77 people to live longer, healthier, better lives. He is a hero to these 77 people, and he is a hero to society. As a heart transplant surgeon, I can attest that there is no better story to capture what was Josiah's favorite phrase, 'Have Heart.'"

SENATOR BILL FRIST, M.D.,
Former U.S. Senate Majority Leader

"Steve and Sarah Berger have faced the worst tragedy imaginable: the tragic death of their son Josiah. There are no words to describe the pain and sense of loss a parent feels when they have lost a child. To say that your world changes forever is an understatement of epic proportions. I know, because our son also died. In fact, it was through our mutual loss that my wife and I became friends with the Bergers. In their new book, *Have Heart*, Steve and Sarah write candidly of what they have experienced. And yet, despite the very real pain they live with each and every day, this book bursts with hope. While no one ever gets over the death of a child, the Bergers are going through this experience with more than their faith intact.

As you will read, their faith is deeper, their insights are more penetrating, and their hope is bright with the expectation of seeing their beloved son again. I trust this book will be a blessing to you."

GREG LAURIE
Senior Pastor, Harvest Christian Fellowship

Unless otherwise noted, all Scripture references are from the New King James Version © 1979, 1980, 1982, 1992 Thomas Nelson, Inc.

Designed and typeset by Koechel Peterson & Associates, Inc., Mpls., MN.

Hand lettering of title and chapter titles by Heather Berger.

ISBN-13: 978-1-936355-03-7

www.HaveHeart.net

CONTENTS

We dedicate this book to the three children we have on earth. Heather, Cody, and Destiny, your faith, strength, compassion, and presence have ministered to your mom and dad more than you will ever know.

We are thrilled about being reunited with Josiah and all of us spending eternity together.

We love you.

ACKNOWLEDGMENTS

TO Vanderbilt Medical Center, thank you for your concern, loving care, and patience with the hundreds of people who chose to pray and worship at all hours of the day and night during our vigil at the hospital.

To the University of Tennessee, particularly W. Timothy Rogers, JD, Vice Chancellor for Student Affairs, thank you for your incredible help and compassion during this time.

To Grace Chapel and its pastors, elders, staff, and leaders, thank you for your nonstop worship, prayer, support, and love.

To Josiah's friends who have continually shown up at our house, thank you for loving us, crying with us, laughing with us, and most importantly, loving Jesus with us.

To the Berger and Benton clans, you all are the best.

To Mark Bright, the fourth Berger brother, your immediate sacrificial response will never be forgotten.

To Wayne Hastings, Allison Allen, and Jennifer Hesse, your contributions made this book a reality.

"In the year that King Uzziah died, I saw the Lord sitting on a throne, high and lifted up, and the train of His robe filled the temple." Sometimes, beloved, it's not until someone we know and love goes to Heaven that we see things that we've never seen before. In a very real sense, we not only feel like Isaiah, but we also feel like the blind man whom Jesus healed. This man testified, "Though I was blind, now I see" (John 9:25). We feel the same way.

Our prayer is that in the midst of your grieving you will see things that you've never seen before and that seeing these things will help your heart find the hope and healing that God alone can bring.

Welcome to our unfolding story.

God Bless,

Steve and Sarah Berger

Have Heart

INTRODUCTION

HEAVENLY JOURNEY

Since our son Josiah went to Heaven, we have developed a brand-new passion and excitement for Heaven, its inhabitants, and its activity. We've come to understand that HEAVEN isn't an indefinable question mark—it's a glorious exclamation point! But before we dig into the exciting realities of Heaven, we need to share a little more about how this journey started for us.

THE PHONE CALL

When Vanderbilt Medical Center was on the other end of the phone, we knew it wasn't good news. In Nashville, Vanderbilt is where the difficult cases go. We've had many calls summoning us to Vanderbilt to comfort and help people in our congregation and other friends. This time it was our turn. Three days after the call from Vanderbilt, on his nineteenth birthday, we released our son Josiah Berger to Heaven.

In the immediate whirlwind surrounding this event, we cried, we remembered, we prayed, and we grieved. Well-meaning people tried to comfort and help us. Many did and many didn't. We spent hours on our faces in prayer for a miracle, but God had other plans. His miracle plan was for others to live through our son's selfless generosity.

As we prayed and studied our Bibles, we came to realize that there was a gulf in our thinking and in the thinking of the church in general. What we heard (and what we continue to hear) from God is that the church doesn't know how to biblically deal with "death." Christians deal with it culturally and traditionally, but we don't deal with it biblically. We regret this fact, and we're committed to helping people get it right and to helping those who are in the depths of grief understand the hope, comfort, and healing that God's Word assures.

Colossians 3:1, 2 says, "If then you were raised with Christ, seek those things which are above, where Christ is, sitting at the right hand of God. Set your mind on things above, not on things on the earth." It's time believers become heavenly minded, and it's time to talk about things that need to be talked about, in the context that they need to be talked about, because we're missing opportunities to receive and share hope. Unfortunately we have moved away from the basic hope that Jesus came to give us—the reality of eternal life with Him in Heaven.

BRIDGING THE GREAT GULF

> *Shall we stop at the poor line, the grave, which all our Christianity is always trying to wipe out and make nothing of, and which we always insist on widening into a great gulf? Shall we not stretch our thought beyond and feel the lifeblood of this holy church, this holy body of Christ, pulsing out into the saints who are living there and coming back throbbing with tidings of their glorious and sympathetic life?[1]*

The quote above is from Right Reverend Phillips Brooks. He went to Heaven when he was fifty-eight years old in the 1800s. He was a great preacher, and it's said of him that his sermons radically influenced Harvard University. He was an Episcopal bishop, and he wrote the lyrics to "O Little Town of Bethlehem."

All the way back in the 1800s, Rt Rev. Brooks wrote about the church's misconception and mishandling of Heaven. He said Christians are always stopping at the grave and trying to widen the gulf between this life and the next. While the truth of Scripture is always trying to make the gulf between this life and the next smaller, we're always trying to widen it. Have we as Christians unknowingly put the sting back into death?

Have we rolled the stone back over Jesus' empty tomb? Does our view of eternal life exclude the Bible's clearly defined concepts of eternal living?

Rt Rev. Brooks wrote that what we should be doing is stretching our thoughts and looking over at the other side of the gulf to see what's going on with the saints in Heaven and then bringing that back and talking about it here on earth. How can we effectively do that if our sights aren't on Heaven and if we don't know what it is or what we'll be doing? The simple answer is, we can't.

A WAKE-UP CALL

Here's a recent, real-life example of how "death" is typically dealt with. A few months before Josiah's accident, I (Steve) was invited to speak at a big Christian high school. I thought, *Sure, I'll go. I'd love to talk to the student body. That would be great.* Obviously, I had no idea what was going to happen in the upcoming months, and I didn't know what God had in store for the student body of that school.

About three weeks after Josiah went to Heaven, there was a terrible car crash, a head-on collision, that involved students from the school. Two of the kids were seriously hurt, and a fourteen-year-old girl instantly went to Heaven. So, here I was, scheduled to speak at this school, and in the midst of preparing to speak there, these two apparently tragic and unrelated events happened.

When I arrived on campus to speak, I began talking to the young man who was in charge of the assembly. I asked him, "What have the speakers been talking about during your student body chapels since the accident?" The young man replied, "Well, the speakers have been talking about, you know, suffering and sorrow and, you know, stuff like that." Then I asked, "Well, has anybody talked about Heaven in the midst of this suffering and sorrow?" And he replied, "No. Nobody's talking about Heaven." I then asked, "Well, did anybody give the opportunity for kids to give their life to Christ, to unpack the reality of how short our lives can be and that we've gotta be right with God?" And the young man replied, "No, there have been no altar calls. We don't really do altar calls here at this [Christian] school."

That's all I needed to hear. I got up and shared what Sarah and I have been learning about Heaven. I shared the biblical perspective on Heaven and what our attitude and response as Christians needs to be. I just wanted to speak truth from God's Word and to give life and hope to hundreds of kids who were there—kids who were heartbroken about their friend, kids who had questions about Heaven. Later, school

Have Heart

leadership said one-third of the school body came to the altar to rededicate or give their heart to Jesus Christ. One-third of the school body! Now, why does that happen? Because our hearts are wired for eternity (Ecclesiastes 3:11). Our hearts want answers; our hearts want hope.

We must learn and talk about Heaven in the midst of suffering. The Curse and suffering are not the final word. Death doesn't have the final authority. This isn't the closing act right here on earth. There's much more to come—infinitely and eternally more. We need to get this right. We must get it right for ourselves, for our own comfort. We must get it right for other people, because they need to hear about the hope of Heaven.

Our minds need to be stretched to the other side. I coined a term to illustrate the need to break out of the box and allow God to maximize our view of Heaven: "sanctified imagination within the confines of biblical truth." Beloved, we need to realize all that God has for us in Heaven. We need to let ourselves be joyful about our future home and the home where our Christian loved ones are right now.

HAVE HEART

*Therefore **we do not lose heart**. Even though our outward man is perishing, yet the inward man is*

being renewed day by day. For our light affliction,
which is but for a moment, is working for us a far
more exceeding and eternal weight of glory, while
we do not look at the things which are seen, but at
the things which are not seen. For the things which
are seen are temporary, but the things which are not
seen are eternal (emphasis added).[2]

Our son had a saying that has come to mean even more to us since his passing: "Have heart." Josiah lived his earthly life to the fullest. He enjoyed being a young man, and he loved Jesus. He encouraged others to have heart when life threw obstacles into their path. Wherever you're at in your journey, we encourage you to have heart.

Our son wanted a tattoo placed over his heart that simply said, "Have." It would have been his way of encouraging himself and others to constantly, no matter the circumstances, have heart and keep going. Although Josiah never received that tattoo, many friends and family members remembered his desire and now have those words tattooed on their bodies to continue the message and share Josiah's story. In a spiritual sense, many more have this written on their hearts. Through this life-changing experience we've had to remember our son's wise counsel, and we encourage you to do the same, in spite of all the pain, anger, frustration, and hopelessness you may be feeling right now. Have heart, Christian—God loves you, His Word is true, and He is very good. Have heart—one day you'll be reunited with your loved one. Have heart—your loved one is more alive and more joyful than ever. Have heart—your loved one's legacy will continue to live here on earth. Have heart—you are not alone. God is in control, and He is ever present and the Master of turning sorrow into joy. God has given us all a gift—the reality of eternal living in Heaven.

Have heart,
Christian—God
loves you, His Word is
true, and He is
very good.

So ready to be outta here!

For to me, to live is Christ,
and to die is gain.

~Philippians 1:21

For the Christian, death is not a tragedy but a
glorious promotion—not the sad end, but the
glorious beginning. Sometimes we hear people say
how sad it is that one should die so young. But that
is a deception of Satan. If a young Christian dies, it
is not sad but glorious. Many of the fairest buds that
ever grew on earth have blossomed in Heaven.[1]

~ Dr. John Rice

Josiah was on his way to beginning his freshman year of college at the University of Tennessee. He couldn't wait to begin this new phase of life, and one day he approached us and said, "I don't want to hurt your feelings, but I am so ready to be outta here!"

We were thinking (and we're sure he was thinking), *It's college*. He was ready to leave the nest and launch out on a new adventure. But now, we look back and think, *Wow, wasn't that interesting?* As we prepared for Josiah to leave for college, I

(Sarah) spoke to the Lord almost every day about my limits. As a mom, I tend toward overparenting, and I did not want to be a "helicopter parent"—always hovering and not allowing for freedom and learning through trial and error. Josiah would have been our second child to leave for college, but this time it would be different. Our first, Heather, remained close in proximity and continued to fellowship with us on Sundays. We were spoiled with her always being near. Josiah, on the other hand, was going to be four hours away and needed a bit more space. Steve and I prayed expectantly that God would show him the way. We simply wanted to do what was right for him and what was right before the Lord.

In reality, the Lord was preparing us for a different type of separation, and obviously in ways we couldn't even imagine, His Holy Spirit was preparing us for that night and the events that have followed.

THE LIFE-CHANGING PHONE CALL

The day was full of preparation and excitement. Josiah was heading to college in just a few days. I (Sarah) had made an oath before the Lord that at any moment if Siah, as we usually call him, asked something of me, I would say yes. When I asked him to feed the dogs, he jokingly answered, "MOJ

(Mother of Josiah), will you go with me? There are spiders out there." He hates spiders! Remembering my promise, I joined Siah in the task. We wrapped our arms around each other as I said, "This will be the last time until Christmas break that we feed the dogs together." He answered, "No, Mom, I will be back for fall break." We hugged and laughed, and I assured him that I understood how eager he was to get "outta here" and that I was excited for him.

Later that night Josiah came downstairs and told me that he was going to meet some friends at a local burger joint. He said it was a little later than he originally thought it would be, but he still wanted to go. I told him, "Honey, you don't have to go." His answer was, "I wouldn't be much of a friend if I didn't go." With that I told him to come over and give me a kiss. That he did gladly, and then he was off.

As we said before, we knew we were in trouble when the call came from Vanderbilt and not our local hospital. We'd been to Vanderbilt many times, and we knew he had been taken there because it was very serious. Then, when they told us he was getting a CAT scan, we knew it was even more serious. We don't know many details of the accident, and we don't feel we need to know. What we do know is that it happened on a winding country road in the fog and less than fifteen minutes from our home. It was a one-car accident, and his body was in perfect condition—not a stitch, nothing broken, except he suffered a serious brain injury.

OUR PRAYERS

For three days, we prayed the Lazarus prayer. In John 11:1–44, we read the story of Lazarus and the desire of Mary and Martha to have Jesus resurrect their brother. He did and that's what we wanted as well. We prayed, "Please, Lord, bring our son back to us. Resurrect him, Lord." But that didn't happen.

We now believe that about twenty minutes after we said good-bye at our home, Siah was in the presence of the heavenly hosts. Days later, after we had fully released Siah to the Lord, a nurse confirmed our discernment that Siah went to Heaven instantly. The nurse told us that the Lord had spoken to him as he read Siah's chart. God said, "You don't have to worry about this one. He is already rejoicing with the angels in Heaven." You see, we were praying the Lazarus prayer for our son, but he was already present with the Lord.

We also prayed the Gethsemane prayer. This was Jesus' prayer in Matthew 26:39 on the night He was betrayed: "O My Father, if it is possible, let this cup pass from Me; nevertheless, not as I will, but as You will." Jesus was willing to submit to God's will for Him, but He asked His Father if there was any other way. But there was not another way for Jesus—He went willingly to the Cross. And there was not another way for us.

We absolutely believe God answers prayers of faith if they are part of His plan. We knew God could raise our son, and we knew He could heal and restore the whole situation. This was absolutely what we and all our friends and family wanted, but that was not God's plan. Although His answer was not what we would have wanted on this side of Heaven, we had to submit ourselves. We truly had to face our faith directly and the idea that our prayers would not be answered the way we wanted. We had to come to grips with God's perfect will and seek His comfort and grace. He has taught us that Josiah's passing wasn't an end, but simply a continuation of His remarkable plan for our son and for us.

Our son expressed his desire to be "outta here." God took a different path than any of us anticipated, and on that path Josiah is ministering and working to help others. He's not doing it in Knoxville at the university as we expected—he's doing it from Heaven! God had a better plan, and our prayers were the first step for us to begin to see it.

Many of you may be praying these same prayers. You want God to change the course of what's happening or has just happened. You may feel shipwrecked, abandoned, and full of questions. Our simple yet profound advice to you is, trust God. Trust Him no matter the outcome. Trust Him because He's good even when we don't understand. *Trust Him.*

THE OUTPOURING

"Hospital." Depending on why you're there, the word itself can mean very different things. If you are the mother of a newborn, it's the place where life begins. If you are the husband of a woman battling multiple sclerosis, it's the place of fight and, hopefully, improvement. If you are the granddaughter of a ninety-year-old grandparent at the end of life on earth, it can be a place of letting go. If you are the parent of a young child receiving treatment for pediatric cancer, it is the place of waiting. Our journey with Josiah in the hospital meant all of those things to our family and friends: the fight, the hope for healing, the place of waiting, and, ultimately, the grief of letting go. What we did not know about Vanderbilt Hospital during those three, arduous days was that it would also become something else to us, something that operates at its best in times of great stress and pain: the church.

Staff at Vanderbilt Medical Center said they had never seen anything like it in all their years of operation. Hundreds of people immediately began showing up at the hospital as soon as the news of Josiah's accident began to circulate. And more were on the way by the time the first morning rolled around. Most times, the chapel was so full that you literally had to crawl over people to move. People were everywhere— on the floor, in the chairs, and on the steps of the small altar.

What we remember more than anything else during those first days were the heartfelt and precious prayers of the people of God. They were all giving voice to the things we were feeling. It was a mix of faith and grief, quiet and petition, hope and sorrow. During those first foggy hours, people we suspect would normally be a bit afraid to talk in a large group grabbed their Bibles and bravely spoke out loud the scriptures God had given them. We can remember Sarah in the front corner, being held together by a group of women. They stroked her hair, covered her with blankets, cried with her, and never left her side. The same thing happened for each of our children. Friends from school, church, and even from out of town moved into the hospital and glued themselves to our kids. Many of our precious family flew in and walked alongside us through the valley that was Vanderbilt Hospital.

After the first day, the number of supporters grew so large that the hospital graciously gave us a group of meeting rooms on the third floor. These rooms became a makeshift church building, cafeteria, and sleeping quarters. At one point, during the first late night, the prayer spilled outside into the courtyard as little groups prayed and worshiped all over. People who were not even connected to Josiah or Grace Chapel were drawn to the outpouring. This gave our folks the opportunity to pray for strangers walking through their own journey of pain and grief.

Sometimes it takes a very difficult thing to strip away all the things we think make us so different from one another. People that might not have known one another at all turned to one another for comfort. Pastors Chris Williamson (Strong Tower Bible Church), Scott Roley (Christ Community Church), and Jeff Dollar (Grace Center) all showed up at the hospital to intercede for our son, for us, and for our church. Impromptu prayer meetings sprung up all over the world.

Our own church, Grace Chapel, held several prayer vigils. One of the church members related to us what she witnessed on her way to one of the vigils. That night Southall Road, the long, country road on which our church sits, was absolutely log-jammed with cars. Hundreds of headlights illuminated the dark path, reminding us that God is our light and our salvation (Psalm 27:1).

One night, after visiting hours had closed, several young

people kept a prayer vigil for our son, walking around the outside of the hospital and praying all through the night. Our church, one that has for years experienced the great goodness of God, plunged headlong into the fellowship of Jesus' sufferings and was made better for it. People's best colors tend to emerge in the fire.

And few shined more beautifully than the staff of Grace Chapel. If they weren't at the hospital, praying with or for us, or praying over Josiah in the ICU, they were selflessly doing the work of the ministry. They kept everything going, even in the middle of their own grief, which was no small thing. They fielded hundreds of phone calls, they responded to the concerns of the church body, they organized prayer meetings and fasts and meals and flowers, and they toted guitars and led worship wherever needed—hospital waiting room or sanctuary prayer vigil. And even when we couldn't bear the agony of it, they stayed right beside our nineteen-year-old son as he went through the organ donation process. Our son was never alone.

Never alone—not even at the scene of the accident. The police were with Josiah immediately. The 911 dispatcher recognized his name and began to pray instantly. She related to us that police and other emergency workers were praying at the site of the accident by the tree and the water. Months later, while speaking at the church of our dear friend, Chris Williamson, we were approached by Aaron Kinney, a former Tennessee Titans football player. After retiring from football, Aaron chose to work with the fire and rescue squad of Williamson County. He was on call the night of our son's accident. He had the difficult job of cutting through the car and freeing Josiah. A follower of Christ literally held our son, prayed for him, carried him, and cared for him—just like Jesus.

Our son was never alone. And if your loved one knew Jesus—even if that decision was made at the last minute—he or she was never alone. Jesus was there. He was there at the scene of the accident. He was there in the halls of the hospital. He was there in the prayers and songs of His people. Wherever His church is—in an ICU unit or in a sanctuary on a Sunday morning—He is there (Matthew 18:20).

THE DONOR REVELATION

On the morning of the second day, faith was high, prayer was nonstop, and worship was passionate. When we awoke on that second day, literally crawling off the conference room floor where we were sleeping, my (Steve's) brother Mike looked at me and said, "The word for today is no." We were not going to accept anything but a miracle. The word for that day was no.

Although we did not relent in asking God for a miracle, we decided it would be prudent to talk with Donor Services because we had so many questions. So, just forty-eight hours after the accident, we began moving toward a decision of donating Josiah's organs, because we knew that's what he would want us to do.

That night, the wonderful people from Donor Services met with us. In our minds, and we'd been preparing for this, we were going to be giving them permission to harvest Josiah's organs at some point. After they sat down, the man opened the file folder he had with him and pulled out a piece of paper. He handed me (Sarah) the paper and said, "As you can see, your son is a donor." I said, "What?!" I thought we were going to be making the hardest decision of our lives. Even though we knew Siah would want to be a donor, it was going to be very difficult to make that decision, especially just two days from the accident.

When the man from Donor Services held up that paper and let us know that Siah had already made that decision, we looked at each other and just said, "We've got to honor Josiah's wishes." The burden of making *the* decision had been lifted.

After discovering that Siah had already made his wishes known, we had to fill out the release forms. The man from Donor Services said, "I'm sorry, but we have about sixty questions to ask you. They are health-related questions." We said, "Okay." I've got to tell you, answering those questions about your beloved son, knowing the potential outcome, is beyond surreal. I wish it upon no one. As we went down through those questions, they were all nos. No, no, no—every single one of them was no.

The word for the day was no, but it wasn't the no we wanted.

We made it through the list of questions, and at the end, we turned to this kind, sweet man from Donor Services and said, "We hope you understand the type of organs you are receiving." And he said, "I'll make sure they know." The words for that day were "no" and "know."

WHISPERING IN JOSIAH'S EAR

The last six months with Josiah were incredible, especially for me (Steve). They were a gift from God, and Sarah and I both recognized that in hindsight. I had the privilege of having some of the deepest conversations with our son about his future, about life, about Christ, about honor, about integrity, and about how to be a man. We know he wasn't perfect. We know he was growing in his faith, but to experience moments where my car turned into a sacred tabernacle and Josiah and I could communicate with the Most High was incredible.

The last in-depth conversation I had with Josiah while he was on this earth was the day before his accident. Our conversation was about his decisions. I told him that it isn't enough to make the right decisions for the moment. I told him that for the rest of his life, it was going to be about *managing* the right decisions. For example, making the decision to follow Christ is not enough—believers must make a lifelong commitment to manage that decision and do the right thing and keep doing the right thing no matter what. Little did I know the decisions Siah would face the very next day.

Josiah has a friend named Dallas, or "Sallad" (Dallas spelled backwards), and Sallad had a dream about Josiah right after the accident. In the dream, Josiah was in his hospital bed. Sallad was watching his friend lying there when the Lord walked into the room and whispered something into our son's ear. Jesus and Josiah had a conversation. When the conversation was over, Sallad said to Jesus, "What did you just say to Siah?" The Lord replied, "That's just between Siah and Me." The dream ended with Josiah getting up and walking out with Jesus. We would have liked for it to have been a walk back to us and to his friends, but instead he got up from his bed and walked with Jesus to his new home, Heaven.

While we were crying out to God in prayer, while we were asking God for a Lazarus miracle, our son was reasoning with his heavenly Father. Would it be best to return to his earthly body or to begin a new adventure in the heavenly realm? There was a battle going on in that hospital room, and we believe Josiah heard his dad's voice saying, "Siah, make right decisions and manage them well. Honor Christ and honor others." I (Sarah), when bedside, continually whispered through tears, "Do what the Father says, Siah. We love you. Do what He says. He knows best." We know Siah heard Jesus saying, "Come, follow Me."

We believe with all our hearts that Jesus laid out the entire plan to our son. "You can go back to your family and friends, or you can come with Me. I'll take care of your folks, and I'll use you for great things." We believe Jesus prepared our son's heart for Heaven—prepared him to say good-bye here on earth so that he would be ready for heavenly life. Jesus promised Josiah that He would take care of his family and friends, and He promised to take care of the seventy-seven people whose lives would be changed by having Josiah's organs.

There were other dreams, too. A lady we never met face-to-face told us that when she heard about Sallad's dream, she realized it aligned with a dream she had had about Josiah. The only difference was that in her dream, when Siah and

Jesus walked out together, Josiah turned to her and said, "Tell Mom and Dad that I love them."

In Idaho, a friend who knew nothing of these dreams was praying for us during the same time that Sallad had his dream. What he heard God saying while he was praying was that there was a battle going on and that decisions were being made. He didn't know about Steve's talk with Siah about making right decisions and managing them. He didn't know we were facing the most difficult decisions in our lives. He didn't know any of this. He just knew what he felt God was telling him—that there was a battle going on and decisions were being made.

This idea of Josiah choosing between earth and Heaven may seem a little strange to you, and we admit that we don't see another instance of it clearly spelled out in Scripture. However, we do believe that this is what happened with our Siah, and we simply want to relay our experiences and what God has revealed to us. Take our experiences for what they are and apply them to your situation as the Holy Spirit guides. We don't claim this scenario plays out the same for everyone, but we do believe this happened with our son.

Because of our son's decision, he is alive in Heaven, and he is alive on earth. His heart is here and is beating in someone's body right now. His organs are here and are helping people live right now. Siah's decision brings us peace, and the peace God has given us "surpasses all understanding" (Philippians 4:7). We know that the only way anyone can have peace is to know Christ, to know His Word, and to completely place his or her life in His arms—to listen when He whispers and follow Him through the door into which He calls.

OUR DECISION

We answered all the donor questions on the night of day two. And on the afternoon of day three, August 14, 2009, the day of Josiah's nineteenth birthday and three days after he entered the hospital, we talked to the chief neurosurgeon at Vanderbilt. He reconfirmed Siah's condition and informed us that there were people waiting, as we spoke, for his organs to literally save their lives.

As a parent, making that decision seventy-two hours after our perfectly healthy, strong, life-in-front-of-him son, who was heading to the University of Tennessee in two days, bounded out the door to meet some friends was beyond surreal.

But everything had changed.

On his nineteenth birthday, we honored Josiah's decision.

The celebration

You are worthy, O Lord, to receive
glory and honor and power; for You
created all things, and by Your
will they exist and were created.

~Revelation 4:11

And I will rise when He calls my name;
No more sorrow, no more pain.
I will rise on eagles' wings;
Before my God fall on my knees.
And rise, I will rise.[1]

~ Chris Tomlin

Josiah's celebration service[2] was a beautiful tribute to Josiah and to God's power, grace, and faithfulness. On that day, we had only just begun to see what God was going to do and will continue to do.

With the sanctuary decorated completely with sunflowers, our worship pastor, Jonathan Allen, began the celebration by singing "I Will Rise" by Chris Tomlin. The first verse says, "There's a peace I've come to know, though my heart and flesh may fail. There's an anchor for my soul; I can say, 'It is well.'

Jesus has overcome, and the grave is overwhelmed. The victory is won; He is risen from the dead."

We were there to celebrate, not a life that was, but a life that is. Josiah is home with Jesus, and we gathered that day to celebrate his life on earth and his eternal life in Heaven that had just begun.

The first scripture from the service was Ephesians 5:14: "Awake, you who sleep, arise from the dead, and Christ will give you light." Josiah would have wanted everyone in the room to know and understand this scripture. In this verse, the voice of Light is speaking to those who are sleeping in darkness and lying in a spiritual funk. The Light calls them to life and illumination. It calls them to live life to the fullest, and if they answer His simple invitation, Christ will shine on them and give them the power they need to have heart and live an abundant life (John 10:10). Two weeks prior to his accident, Josiah told us, "Sleep is a complete waste of time." He was a young man who never wasted a minute of his life. He was fully alive on earth, and now, he is fully alive in Heaven and encouraging others to awake, arise, and receive the Light.

It was incredible to see over two thousand people at Josiah's memorial service. We filled the sanctuary plus six overflow rooms. There were so many cars that we had to use the front lawn, a rather large, open section, for auxiliary parking. There were people watching from all over the world via the Internet. People as far away as Egypt and Sri Lanka, as well as people from all around the United States, were a part of this service, and hundreds received Christ as a result of Josiah's legacy. The celebration was a wake-up call.

Like Jesus at Lazarus's funeral, we asked those in attendance, "Do you believe?" We wanted people to be able to respond to the wake-up call and to what we talked about in the last chapter—making good decisions and managing them for life. We made the call, and hundreds of people of all ages came forward to either receive Christ for the first time or to recommit their lives to Him.

Josiah's legacy began with organ donation and continued with the challenge for people to wake up, have heart, and come forward to make the right decision. To see this response to Christ has helped us greatly to overcome the price we paid.

How these people responded to the accident and Josiah's life celebration service changed our vantage point. We caught, from these faithful people, a glimpse of Heaven to come. We could tangibly see nonstop, active prayer and worship, and we knew that our son was doing that in Heaven. His legacy contributed to our own sense of peace and perseverance. His legacy brought people to their knees, asking for miracles and worshiping God. It radically changed us. It radically helped us to see this outpouring of genuine worship.

The accident and the celebration made the nightly news. Josiah's life continued to affect people, and it continues today as he's participating from Heaven (we'll speak to this in the coming chapters).

THE MYSTERY PAINTING

As a grieving father and mother, it's vitally important for us to understand our son's legacy, his presence, and his activity in Heaven. Josiah's legacy continues to minister to us. People all around us have enjoyed wonderful experiences and dreams involving Josiah. We receive a huge amount of comfort from their experiences, and it's beautiful to us how all the things that have happened have come randomly from people who have never shared or compared notes or talked to one another. It's God's spontaneous sovereignty that He allows gifts from the land of the living, Heaven, to touch those in the land of the dying, this earth, to bring comfort and peace.

We call these gifts "God Nods." Let's take a minute and clearly define this for you because this is an important part of your healing journey. A God Nod is affirmation and direction.

It's God affirming that you are on His radar and haven't been forgotten. It's God directing you to pay attention and look deeper. It's God saying, "Check this out." With that being said, be on the lookout for God Nods. They'll be happening when you least expect them. They cause healing. Don't miss them. We'd like to share one God Nod in particular that happened to us that shows how deeply God cares for us.

The day of Josiah's life celebration service, we were looking at some pictures. A few hours before the celebration was to begin, I (Steve) came across a picture that Sarah had taken of Josiah at his grandparents' house in Three-Arch Bay in Laguna Beach, CA. I e-mailed the picture to our Executive Pastor, Jim Sterling, and said, "This is the picture we want on the screen—no others."

Jim was working on a montage of pictures to be shown during the service, but my e-mail changed the direction. This picture, with Josiah's arms outstretched overlooking the Pacific Ocean, was to be the picture used. It's a pose of worship, humility, and surrender.

A short time before the service was scheduled to start, Jim walked through the sanctuary to check on last-minute details. As he walked toward the front of the church, there, leaning against the altar, was an unsigned painting of *that* photograph. Sarah and I had only run across it a few minutes before we e-mailed it to Jim. The only difference between the photo and the painting was that in the painting, Josiah appeared to be transparent. It spoke to us, as if Josiah was saying, "I am here; you just can't see me."

There were only two or three people in the sanctuary at the time. None of them claimed it was their work. We have no idea where it came from or who painted it. It was just there for us. We don't even know how anyone outside of just a few people ever saw this particular photograph of our son. It was a mystery, it was a miracle, and it was a gift. To this day, we do not know who painted Josiah's picture.

In the midst of our deepest grief, God gave us a gift. He gave us a special nod.

We mention this for several reasons. One is to encourage you to look for God Nods. Be on the lookout for those special things that only God can do (and He can do amazing things in so many ways, as you'll see). Please don't let anger, bitterness, unknowing, or doubt prevent you from seeing the blessings of God in the midst of your pain and suffering.

We also share this as one other example of legacy. Whether it's an organ donation, a conversion, or a painting, our son lives and his legacy continues.

We firmly believe that ours is not just an isolated case. Every believer who passes on to Christ's arms leaves a legacy, and the legacy continues. Keep that close to your heart, and train your eyes to see your loved one's legacy and the God Nods He provides.

Brokenheartedness

is way beyond

just having a

bad day...

Turning your mourning into dancing

He heals the brokenhearted and
binds up their wounds.

~Psalm 147:3

Out of these ashes
Beauty will rise,
And we will dance among the ruins.
We will see it with our own eyes.
Out of this darkness
New light will shine,
And we'll know the joy that's coming in the morning.
In the morning
Beauty will rise.

~ Steven Curtis Chapman[1]

UNDERSTANDING BROKENHEARTEDNESS

We have a God who loves us, cares for us, and meets us face-to-face in our darkest hour and deepest need. If you get one thing from this chapter, this is what is most important for you to completely understand—not just with your head, but also with your heart, as broken as it might be right now.

Brokenheartedness is way beyond just having a bad day or going through a tough season. Rest assured that God is there for those times as well, but we're talking about a life-changing, soul-wrenching tragedy in which every other trial, every other heartbreak you've faced suddenly pales in comparison. Brokenheartedness can be caused by any number of things, and each person's story is unique.

Brokenheartedness is when your heart is obliterated, scattered, and devastated. When your heart is broken, you wonder if it can ever be put back together again or if you'll ever pull out of this thing. It's when your faith and trust are stretched and attacked like no other time. Steven Curtis Chapman, after his precious little girl Maria went to Heaven, said it so clearly to us: "There will be times when you'll question everything you believe." No matter how much faith you had before your heart was broken, the Enemy will use your brokenheartedness as an opportunity to attack you ferociously.

Although the cause of brokenheartedness varies, the symptoms are similar, and the solution is always the same. We must cling to the fact that Jesus came to heal the brokenhearted. He didn't just come to cheer us up on a sad day. He came so that He could show us power and healing when our hearts are in little pieces and scattered all over the place. He came so we could literally "have heart"! He came for THAT.

Solomon, the king who sought wisdom, recognized the utter devastation of a broken heart. He wrote in Proverbs 18:14, "The spirit of a man will sustain him in sickness, but who can bear a broken spirit?" Your spirit can pull you out of a bad day, but what about when your spirit is scattered? What happens when your heart is obliterated? Solomon asked, "Can anyone bear that?"

We are here to tell you, "YES, YOU CAN BEAR IT!" You can bear it because of the grace, power, peace, love, compassion, presence, and promises of Jesus Christ. That's the only way you can bear brokenheartedness. Yes, it seems unbearable at times. Yes, it's hard, but Jesus came so all of us can have heart and be made whole again (Luke 4:18). Jesus Himself revives the hearts of hurting people, and He is the solution to our suffering. Draw near to Him, because He has drawn near to you.

NO ONE IS EXEMPT

When tragedy strikes, far too often we ask why or question God's presence, love, or wisdom in allowing this thing to happen. Or we may say, "This isn't fair" or "This isn't right." Somehow this kind of thinking has crept into our minds, and it goes something like this: "We're Christians and we should be exempt from brokenheartedness." This simply isn't true.

We want to say boldly and compassionately that the church needs to wake up and grow up—brokenheartedness can happen to anyone at anytime.

First Corinthians 13:11, 12 says, "When I was a child, I spoke as a child, I understood as a child, I thought as a child; but when I became a man, I put away childish things. For now we see in a mirror, dimly, but then face-to-face. Now I know in part, but then I shall know just as I also am known." We need to put away these immature, childish notions that we are somehow exempt from suffering and let mature thinking prepare us for when the rug is pulled out from underneath us. We need to be prepared for that moment, because it's foolishness to follow the lie that nothing bad will ever happen to believers. We all need the truth to stand on should tragedy strike.

Unheavenly things happen on earth to believers and unbelievers alike. There is no discrimination. Anyone, in just a second, can have a broken heart. We need to settle this misconception of exemption in advance, when life is going great, so that we're prepared should God allow heartbreak in our life. Not being prepared for the possibility of grief and suffering opens the door to a whole host of whys, and on this side of the thin veil, we'll never get satisfactory answers to why our hearts were broken—you won't and we won't.

A pastor friend of ours had some invaluable wisdom for us within days of Josiah going to Heaven. He told us, "You can't ask why and let why dominate your thoughts. You can't let the 'whys' replace the 'knows' of your life. All the whys will never be answered this side of Heaven." Looking for answers to the whys will only add another layer to your grief and will stall the healing Jesus wants to bring. If you are clinging to pain until you know why, you must throw your whys to the wind.

Instead of clinging to pain, we must cling to God's love and settle in our hearts and minds that we know where to go for reprieve and remedy—God's Word. What we know is that "God is love" (1 John 4:8). What we know is that nothing can "separate us from the love of God" (Romans 8:38, 39). What we know is that He makes "everything beautiful in its time" (Ecclesiastes 3:11). What we know is that He will "not leave you nor forsake you" (Deuteronomy 31:8). What we know is that He is "near to those who have a broken heart" (Psalm 34:18). What we know is that He does "all things well" (Mark 7:37).

Consider this account in Matthew's Gospel:

> *Therefore whoever hears these sayings of Mine,*
> *and does them, I will liken him to a wise man who*
> *built his house on the rock: and the rain descended,*

> *the floods came, and the winds blew and beat on*
> *that house; and it did not fall, for it was founded on*
> *the rock. But everyone who hears these sayings of*
> *Mine, and does not do them, will be like a foolish*
> *man who built his house on the sand: and the rain*
> *descended, the floods came, and the winds blew and*
> *beat on that house; and it fell. And great was its fall.²*

Did you notice that the rains fell, the floods came, the winds blew, and the elements beat on *both* of the houses? It happens to both the wise and the foolish, the saint and the sinner alike.

The issue is, will you fall or stand in the midst of your brokenness? It all depends on you responding to God's truth. If you respond with faith, trust, and obedience, you will stand, and you will make it. Trust us, this is what we've chosen to do, and as you'll see, we've seen God at work in mighty ways in the midst of our pain and suffering. If you respond with doubt, anger, and self-pity, you will fall, and you won't make it. You won't have the truth to guide you.

JESUS CAME TO HEAL THE BROKENHEARTED

This is good news: Jesus came to heal the brokenhearted! Please don't look at this as just a nice greeting card sentiment. It's not sentimental—it's supernatural. Through the prophet

Ezekiel, God penned these words about Himself: "I will seek what was lost and bring back what was driven away, bind up the broken and strengthen what was sick" (34:16). The solution for brokenheartedness is not a program—it's a Person, and His name is Jesus Christ. He is the solution to humanity's brokenness. Jesus binds up broken hearts and causes them to be strong again, to live and pump vitality into our lives.

The very Person of Jesus is in the trenches of our grief, and He is the solution to our broken hearts. After Jesus' friend Lazarus passed away, Jesus went to Bethany to comfort Mary and Martha, Lazarus's sisters. When He saw the place where Lazarus was buried, He wept and grieved with the family and friends (John 11:35). Jesus came into the closeness of Mary and Martha's grief. His weeping and His love surrounded them. It shows the character, love, and nearness of Christ. It's a clear picture of Christ's heart for you as you are grieving.

Jesus came to display His love and compassion and to bind our hearts back together, even in the worst of the worst. He's here to bring healing and to pick up all those tiny, scattered bits of your heart and bind them back together—to make your heart whole again. How precious is that? We need to know this ourselves, and we need to communicate this incredible truth with compassion to others who have broken hearts.

No matter how broken, scattered, obliterated, and devastated you are right now, know that you are not beyond Jesus' healing touch. Jesus created your heart, and He can heal your heart. Cry out to Jesus, and let Him start the process of healing. It's His specialty.

GOD'S TRUTH IS THE FOUNDATION

God is there waiting for you. He's there to start the healing process. He's waiting for you with comfort and truth in the Person of the Holy Spirit. John 16:7, 13 says, "Nevertheless I tell you the truth. It is to your advantage that I go away; for if I do not go away, the Helper will not come to you; but if I depart, I will send Him to you. However, when He, the Spirit of truth, has come, He will guide you into all truth."

God has given His children a Comforter who guides us into His truth. If you feel disconnected from God's comfort and truth, the Holy Spirit may be the missing link for you. We would encourage you to ask the Holy Spirit to come in and fill you with God's truth. The Comforter will serve and soothe you as Jesus picks up the bits of your heart and carries you through the healing process.

From the beginning of our pain, we asked the Lord for only His truth. We didn't want to be comforted by a lie or counterfeit sympathies. We wanted God and His truth. We quickly learned that something temporary only comforts for a moment, but God's Comforter gives something eternal in His truth.

The Holy Spirit also convicts believers of what is true and what is not. He is the ultimate Teacher and Comforter. In His comforting, He brings not only the truth, but He also proves God's Word time and time again in our hearts. This was certainly true for us. In the time of our deepest need, all the scriptures we had bathed and marinated in for years became so precious and powerful. When the Holy Spirit brings those scriptures to mind, we can put the full weight of our trust on them. Because of this focus on truth, we will not listen to the doubt and negativity that Satan whispers in our ears. No, we will not be overcome—we will be overcomers.

King David wrote in Psalm 34:18, "The LORD is near to those who have a broken heart, and saves such as have a contrite spirit." When our hearts are broken and we feel that God isn't near, the truth tells us He is. When we feel like God's forsaken us, the truth tells us He's nearer than at any other time in our lives. This is the truth we need to meditate on, claim, speak, and thank God for.

Note in the verse that "LORD" is spelled in small caps.

This has a purpose. Bible translators use caps and small caps to identify where the covenant name of God (or YHWH, phonetically pronounced "Yahweh") appears in the text. The Bible describes Yahweh as the one true God who met Moses at the burning bush, delivered Israel from Egypt, and gave Moses the Ten Commandments. In this psalm, David was talking about "the great I AM" (Exodus 3:14), the Creator God who is self-sufficient, all-powerful, and self-existent. He is the First and the Last, the Alpha and the Omega.

In writing this psalm, David could have chosen other names for God. For example, he could have chosen "Adonai" (meaning "my Lord"), but he didn't. He could have used "Elohim" (meaning "He is the power over powers"), but he did not. He said, "Lord," the great "I AM." He used the name of God that is too big for words, and beloved, that is the God who is near to the brokenhearted. That's a promise we need to hold on to when we are brokenhearted, and it's a promise we need to share with those who are hurting around us.

Paul wrote in Romans 8:38, 39, "For I am persuaded that neither death nor life, nor angels nor principalities nor powers, nor things present nor things to come, nor height nor depth, nor any other created thing, shall be able to separate us from the love of God which is in Christ Jesus our Lord."

He is saying that the love of God hasn't stopped. It didn't stop when Jesus was on the Cross, it didn't stop when Paul had his head pressed against a stone table before he was beheaded, and it didn't stop when Peter was hanging upside down to be crucified. The love of God never, ever stops in the midst of our brokenheartedness, and regardless of what we feel, we must hold on to this—*nothing* can separate us from God's incredible, unbelievable love for us.

You might say, "God, if you loved me this would not have happened," and you would be mistaken. If you question God's never-ending love and allow yourself to dwell on that thought, you are going to sink. God's love never stops. His love is near, because He is near and He is faithful. Believing this fact and letting it constantly bubble up will strengthen and encourage and comfort you. This is the truth, and the truth you know will set you free—and keep you free (John 8:32). When you are brokenhearted, every bit of truth you think you know will be challenged, and you must hold on to the truth of God's love like nothing you've ever held on to in your entire life. *Nothing* separates us from God's love.

Paul said in Ephesians 3:20 that God is "able to do exceedingly abundantly above all that we ask or think, according to the power that works in us." If you feel, even for one second, that you might never recover from your brokenheartedness, remember that God is able to do way more than you can ever imagine. We need to be rooted and grounded in this truth so that no matter how hard the wind blows, we'll stand.

There are glorious and wonderful things happening in the midst of our brokenness (we'll share some later in the book), and believe it or not, there are wonderful things God can do in your brokenness, too. But you have to be willing to have heart and give your heart to God and His truth. There is tremendous risk in not doing this. The risk is clinging to something that is untrue and not from the Spirit. For the brokenhearted, there are times when being healed is unimaginable, but God can do the unimaginable—He does it every day. God wants to do something incredible and beautiful in your life. God wants to turn your mourning into dancing.

YOU MUST WANT TO BE HEALED

You might be asking, "*Want* to be healed? Who wouldn't want to be healed from a broken heart?" The answer is, plenty of people. That's right, there are many people who don't want to be healed because their broken heart has become their identity. It's many people's way to receive temporary, powerless pity from other people. They want to be known as people who have never recovered but made the best of a bad situation. They love to be with people who appeal to their carnal psyche and victim mentality rather than the Spirit of God and His truth.

The apostle John wrote about one such person:

> *Now there is in Jerusalem by the Sheep Gate a pool, which is called in Hebrew, Bethesda, having five porches. In these lay a great multitude of sick people, blind, lame, paralyzed, waiting for the moving of the water. For an angel went down at a certain time into the pool and stirred up the water; then whoever stepped in first, after the stirring of the water, was made well of whatever disease he had. Now a certain man was there who had an infirmity thirty-eight years. When Jesus saw him lying there, and knew that he already had been in that condition a long time, He said to him, "Do you want to be made well?"*
>
> *The sick man answered Him, "Sir, I have no man to put me into the pool when the water is stirred up; but while I am coming, another steps down before me."*
>
> *Jesus said to him, "Rise, take up your bed and walk." And immediately the man was made well, took up his bed, and walked. And that day was the Sabbath.[3]*

It's our opinion that this fellow didn't want to be made well. For thirty-eight years he was there, and in all that time he could not find one person to push him into the pool before somebody else got into it? Thirty-eight years?

Jesus had to ask this guy if he wanted to be healed because some people don't want to be. In your brokenness, you have a decision to make—do you want man's pity or God's healing? We had to make that same decision, and thank God, we made it very early. So, what will your decision be? Will you cling to your brokenness or surrender to God's everlasting peace, comfort, and healing? You cannot ride the fence on this one, and we would encourage you with everything we have not to settle for man's pity. It's easy to get addicted to it, but it is a cheap imitation. Choose God's love, His truth, and His comfort over anything else. If you know you want to be healed but don't know where to start, simply cry out to God for His help and His truth. He knows all the places where your heart is scattered, and if you want Him to, He'll bind them up for you.

Before we move on, we want to clearly dispel the myth that by embracing healing, you are somehow diminishing the tragedy that caused your heart to break in the first place. Satan wants you to hold on to your pain and brokenness, so he is going to whisper lies in your ear at every turn. He'll say, "You know, if you open your heart to Jesus, if you open yourself up to healing, you're going to start forgetting your loved one.

It will almost be as if that person never existed if you allow yourself to feel alive again. You don't want to make your loved one's life seem small and unimportant, do you? Hold on to that pain just a little longer . . . just a little longer."

Satan is the father of lies (John 8:44), and you need to know that healing does not make your loved one or your tragedy small or insignificant. Embrace the healing that Jesus came to bring, and don't let Satan's lies twist the work Jesus wants to do in your heart.

*God wants us to fully
understand His power,
His beauty, His majesty,
and His will.*

Heaven Revealed

"Eye has not seen, nor ear heard,
nor have entered into the heart of man the things
which God has prepared for those who love Him."
But God has revealed them to us through His Spirit.
For the Spirit searches all things,
yes, the deep things of God.

~1 Corinthians 2:9, 10

For all I know, what looks like goin' away may be
a comin' nearer. And there may be ways of comin'
nearer to one another yonder that we know nothing
about down here.[1]

~ George MacDonald

As we said in the last chapter, the grief of brokenheartedness is something that is indescribable. We grieve deeply and have spent many days and nights soaking the carpet with tears as we cry out to God. We do not grieve for a son who is lost. No, we know where Josiah is. We grieve because we dearly miss his physical presence with us. We miss face time with our boy. What has kept us sane is the knowledge that Josiah is alive in Heaven (not dead or lost) and that we are bound together eternally. That's amazing comfort for the grieving. In the book *A Glimpse of Heaven*, Lutheran minister Reverend F. R. Anspach is quoted as saying:

> I will not deplore you [talking about his family members who passed on to Heaven] as lost; for ye are still ours, we are yet one, and shall forever be, for that bond that unites us shall exist in all its vigor when the wheels of the universe stand still! When every mountain shall have fallen, it shall stand unimpaired; when every law whose authority is acknowledged by material nature shall have been annulled, this law which makes us one, shall be in force.[2]

The Reverend Anspach is right on. And in the midst of our grief, we have asked the Holy Spirit to reveal to us the "deep things of God," as 1 Corinthians 2:9, 10 suggests. We've found hope and encouragement in what He's revealed to us.

GOD IS GOOD AND HIS WORD IS TRUE

When it comes to Heaven, not only are there some holes in many churches' teaching, but there are also many Christians who are grieving and who have questions that are not being answered. This can be paralyzing to someone who is grieving. Since Josiah's accident we've received so many questions from people. This e-mail came to us just a few short days ago from this writing:

> Hi there. My son recently passed away, and I have many questions if you would be willing to e-mail me back. I am not sure where to start, so I'll just ask in no order. Some [questions] sound stupid to me, but I hope not to you.
>
> > Can my son hear me when I talk to him?
> >
> > Is he always around me, and can he see me?
> >
> > Is there any good way to communicate with him?
> >
> > Will he come to visit me? Or do you believe in us getting signs?
>
> I have a lot of anger, and I don't know how to make it go away. It's just not fair. I was told I can't let the "why" take over me, but I can't help but want to know, "Why my son? Why so soon?" Will I ever get that answer? When I am reunited with him [in Heaven], will I be able to stand before God and get that answer?[3]

The next few chapters will give answers to these and many other questions. We'll start with some things you may not have heard or thought about before.

THINGS REVEALED

Scripture reveals so much to us at various times and in various ways. How many times have you read a familiar passage and realized you just learned something new and different? The Holy Bible is alive. It's fresh and always revealing new things to us through God's Spirit. As we shared at the beginning of the chapter, 1 Corinthians 2:9, 10 tells us: "But as it is written: 'Eye has not seen, nor ear heard, nor have entered into the heart of man the things which God has prepared for those who love Him.' But God has revealed them to us through His Spirit. For the Spirit searches all things, yes, the deep things of God."

Many times we just focus on verse 9 and ignore verse 10, but we can't do that. It reminds us that God is revealing things to us through His Spirit and that the Spirit searches all things—even tragedies and the deep things of God. He's there to reveal these deeper things to us. God has one goal when He speaks to us. He wants us to fully understand what He's saying and the meaning of what He is saying. Verse 10 tells us that He has sent a special Person, the Holy Spirit, to help us make sense of Scripture and of what He is saying. Remember, anything we think God is saying or revealing must line up with the Word and the nature, character, and will of God.

God wants us to understand all there is about Him. He wants us to fully understand His power, His beauty, His majesty, and His will. He also wants us to understand the plans He has for us (Jeremiah 29:11) and the position we have in Christ (Ephesians 2:6). Nothing is hidden; there are no secret agendas with God. He reveals deep things, and we will find them by seeking and searching His Word.

ANSWERS GIVEN

We've had, and continue to have, plenty of "what" (not "why") questions for God. Fortunately, we have a patient, loving, and understanding Father who has all the answers. He gives us answers in many ways and in many forms, and for that we are eternally grateful. Matthew 7:11 says, "If you then, being evil, know how to give good gifts to your children, how much more will your Father who is in heaven give good things to those who ask Him!" This passage focuses on the answering and providing Father. Parents want to give their children good gifts, and since God loves us unimaginably, how much more could He give us if we just asked?

As we began asking questions, God gave us many good gifts. Believe us, we had questions just like the mother's e-mail we shared in this chapter. We decided to turn to Scripture and boldly ask God for answers, and He graciously, lovingly, and patiently gave them to us.

Isaiah 6:1–4 says:

> In the year that King Uzziah died, I saw the Lord sitting on a throne, high and lifted up, and the train of His robe filled the temple. Above it stood seraphim; each one had six wings: with two he covered his face, with two he covered his feet, and with two he flew. And one cried to another and said: "Holy, holy, holy is the Lord of hosts; the whole earth is full of His glory!" And the posts of the door were shaken by the voice of him who cried out, and the house was filled with smoke.

Sometimes it takes the passing of a loved one for us to clearly see heavenly things. In these verses, the prophet admits that he saw the Lord and some very unusual-looking seraphim after the death of the king. The passing of King Uzziah triggered a bigger event. It gave Isaiah answers and a vision of Heaven. We can't help but wonder what some of Isaiah's friends must have thought about his out-of-the-ordinary, supernatural experience. Was he delusional? Hysterical? Or worse, heretical? By sharing this supernatural experience, he was taking tremendous risk, while at the same time communicating what God had shown him about Heaven and its inhabitants that he'd never seen before. Like Isaiah, we're willing to share our ongoing experience, risking the potential ridicule of some in order to bring hope to the hurting.

HOPE RESTORED

Sometimes parents need a sign of God's goodness from Heaven, the land of the living. Sometimes the grief is so all-encompassing that we need a place to go to find hope and some rest from the grief. Second Corinthians 4:16–18 tells us,

> *Therefore we do not lose heart. Even though our outward man is perishing, yet the inward man is being renewed day by day. For our light affliction, which is but for a moment, is working for us a far more exceeding and eternal weight of glory, while we do not look at the things which are seen, but at the things which are not seen. For the things which are seen are temporary, but the things which are not seen are eternal.*

God, through the writing of the apostle Paul, tells us to have heart. Sure, we are grief stricken—who wouldn't be? But through it all, God is revealing and giving us hope day by day (and sometimes minute by minute).

Our grief, as paralyzing as it is sometimes, is really a "light affliction" when compared to what God has for us and for our loved ones who have passed on to Heaven. When we look at only what we can see, we're blind to the eternal—those things that are unseen. When our bitterness, anger, doubt, and unknowing blinds us, we cannot see God's gifts to us, and we cannot hear God's voice when He comes to comfort, soothe, and give us answers.

We discovered that we must try as best we can to look at the eternal things that God has promised. Our hope can be restored when we focus on Him and His eternal place, Heaven.

Hazel Felleman wrote:

> Think of—
> Stepping on shore, and finding it Heaven!
> Of taking hold of a hand, and finding it God's hand.
> Of breathing a new air, and finding it celestial air.
> Of feeling invigorated, and finding it Immortality.
> Of passing from storm to tempest to an unknown
>   calm.
> Of waking up, and finding it Home.[4]

HEAVEN'S GLORIES

Heaven is a beautiful place with no sin, no unrest, and the unlimited love of God. When we understand Heaven's glories, no wonder the apostle Paul said it's gain to go there. He wrote in Philippians 1:21–23, "For to me, to live is Christ, and to die is gain. But if I live on in the flesh, this will mean fruit from my labor; yet what I shall choose I cannot tell. For I am hard-pressed between the two, having a desire to depart and be with Christ, which is far better."

Regarding Paul's words in this passage, R. C. Sproul wrote:

> *Paul does not despise life in this world. He says that he is "hard pressed" between choosing to remain and desiring to depart. The contrast he points to between this life and heaven is not a contrast between the bad and the good. The comparison is between the good and the better. This life in Christ is good. Life in heaven is better. Yet he takes it a step farther. He declares that to depart and be with Christ is far better (verse 23). The transition to heaven involves more than a slight or marginal improvement. The gain is great. Heaven is far better than life in this world.[5]*

Paul understood the glories of Heaven. He knew that being with the Father was far, far better than anything he could do on earth. Paul also made it clear that people can only say "to die is gain" when they have lived their life committed to Jesus Christ. When people live their life for Jesus, we don't have to, and we should not, grieve over their passing. We can grieve over our pain. We sorrow, but our sorrow should not be as those who have no hope; we sorrow because we miss them. But we don't sorrow for them. We don't grieve for them. For if a person is living for Christ, to die is gain, and to see our loved ones go into the arms of Jesus is gain as well. Believers have the hope and assurance of Heaven's surpassing glories!

NO CONFUSION

Author and teacher Dr. Bruce Lockerbie and his wife Lory wrote this about the hope Christians have:

> Christians don't need to live like losers in some vast cosmic dice game. Christians are never victims; in fact, Christians need never be either pessimistic or optimistic, as though somehow their ultimate destiny were still in doubt. For a Christian, the truly Biblical virtue is hopefulness because our hope is secure in the promises of Jesus Christ, who has set us free from the fear of death.[6]

Hopefulness, not fear. Hopefulness, not doubt.

The apostle Paul was so adamant about this issue of Heaven that he said something that sounds even a bit harsh or degrading. In 1 Thessalonians 4:13 Paul wrote to the believers in Thessalonica: "I do not want you to be ignorant, brethren, concerning those who have fallen asleep [passed on to Heaven], lest you sorrow as others who have no hope."

Paul was saying, "Hey, man, I don't want you to be ignorant about people who have passed on into glory. I don't want you to be confused. It affects how you grieve." Ignorance or confusion about this issue of physical death and Heaven leads to sorrow without hope. Sorrow without hope leads to anger, doubt, and confusion.

Unfortunately, when it comes to grieving, believers are often no better off than the people of the world, but it shouldn't be that way. Many believers are confused or just don't know heavenly truths. When we understand what Heaven really is all about, we can be sorrowful in a way that's filled with hope, not despair.

The reality and truth of Heaven has gotten us up in the morning. It has moved us out of our bed and has kept us from probably going insane. Have we sorrowed? Do we cry? Absolutely. But it's never one time been out of anger or disgust or hopelessness or going, "God, where's my son?" We do not view Josiah's passing as a tragic loss, nor do we ever refer to him as "lost" or "dead." The Bible, in Philippians 1:21, reminds us that Heaven is gain, not loss. We know where Siah is—in the presence of Jesus, His loving Savior! Siah's earthly body may be dead, but his heavenly body is fully alive, active, and aware. Believers will "never die" (John 11:26)—it's not over when they pass on to Heaven and into Jesus' arms. They live! Siah lives. He is still part of our family, and he is still our brother in Christ, alive in Heaven with the rest of the saints and angels and God Almighty.

So our sorrow has always been filled with hope, and there's no confusion. We sorrow because of the simple fact that we miss our son. Frankly, we don't expect that's ever going to change. If we could stop missing our boy, something would be wrong. So we miss him. But, and here's the point: we don't miss him into hopelessness. We still cry often, and sometimes it's a struggle, but we don't cry tears of hopelessness. Many times, our tears are out of gratitude for the reality of Heaven and our Christ, who loved us enough to give His life so that we could live, not only with Him forever, but also with our loved ones forever. Thank You, Lord.

The simple truth is that God, in His way and in His time and through His Word, reveals special things to us. He gives us answers to our questions as long as we keep asking. He's patient and stands ready to direct us, gently lead us, and respond to us.

They are alive

For we who are in
this tent groan, being burdened,
not because we want to be unclothed,
but further clothed, that mortality
may be swallowed up by life.

~ 2 Corinthians 5:4

It is not death to die
To leave this weary road,
And midst the brotherhood on high
To be at home with God

It is not death to close
The eye long dimmed by tears,
And wake, in glorious repose,
To spend eternal years

It is not death to bear
The wrench that sets us free
From dungeon chain, to breathe the air
Of boundless liberty.

It is not death to fling
Aside this sinful dust
And rise, on strong exulting wing
To live among the just.

Jesus, Thou Prince of Life,
Thy chosen cannot die:
Like Thee, they conquer in the strife
To reign with Thee on high.

~ Henri Malan

E vangelist D. L. Moody said, "Someday you will read in the papers that Moody is dead. Don't you believe a word of it. At that moment I shall be more alive than I am now. I was born of the flesh in 1837, I was born of the spirit in 1855. That which is born of the flesh may die. That which is born of the Spirit shall live forever."[1]

Moody was right on. He knew the Bible. It's unfortunate, but some scriptures don't mean anything until we need them, and for all of us, this time of grieving is that time to be immersed in God's Word. One of the things we've learned from the Scriptures is that, without a doubt, our loved ones in Heaven are fully alive, active, and aware. Yes, our loved ones are alive—just in a different place. Henry Morris, from the Institute for Creation Research, wrote this about the fact that Heaven is a literal place and filled with saints who are fully alive:

> *"And it came to pass, as they still went on, and talked, that, behold, there appeared a chariot of fire, and horses of fire, and parted them both asunder; and Elijah went up by a whirlwind into heaven"*
> *(II Kings 2:11).*

This remarkable event—the translation of Elijah alive into heaven, without dying—was incredible. It was miraculous, but it really happened! Among other things, it assures us that heaven is a real place in this created universe, for Elijah is still there in his physical body, still alive, to this very day.[2]

A SHOWER COMPLAINT

Very shortly after Josiah passed, I (Steve) had an immediate, burgeoning sense of Heaven and eternity. I knew immediately where Josiah was. He wasn't lost to me. I knew he was experiencing things so inexpressibly beautiful and mysterious that, given the choice to return, I don't believe he would have. He's more alive than any of us have ever been on our very best day. More alive than on the day I met Jesus. Or on the day I married my bride, his mother, Sarah. More alive than on the day I held him in my arms as my firstborn son or on the days I held his brother and sisters. More alive than on the day I was called into the ministry. More alive than I was on all of those amazing days is my son right now. Siah is a part of my past, present, and an even bigger part of my future. I knew all these things in a deeper way than I have known most things, even very early on.

Sometimes, though, all the truth in the world doesn't stop the hurting. We hurt with hope, to be sure, but we still hurt.

We have to be prepared for that reality as we walk through the valley of the shadow of death. We have to know that, on some days, our job will be to grieve. And as we do the necessary work of grieving, answers will sometimes appear to remind us that this valley walk will not last forever. I recall a particularly difficult part of the journey through the valley just days after Josiah went to Heaven:

> As a dad, I was looking forward to sharing certain milestones in my Siah's life. College, marriage, children. I dreamed of standing proudly by as Josiah received his diploma from the University of Tennessee. I wanted to officiate my son's marriage to his bride. And I definitely longed to hold Josiah's children—children that would have been our grandchildren. I remember puzzling over these thoughts, agonizing over them. And early one morning still turning these issues over and around in my mind, I finally poured out my complaint before the Lord (Psalm 142:2). I did all this in the shower. The shower is a fabulous place to get real. In the shower, I could sob and heave and cry out, unconcerned about being heard. In the shower, my tears and the water could run together. In the shower, I could come undone. And, believe me, I did.
>
> "What about college? What about marriage? What about children? What about all the things he will

*never, ever experience this side of Heaven? What
about those things, Lord?" I sobbed out questions
that were some of the most emotionally charged I
have ever asked aloud in my whole life. And there, in
my bathroom shower, hidden away from everyone
else but God, I finally heard the Lord speak.*

"I have more than made up for these things."

*I was stunned to silence. All I heard was the sound of
water. After a minute, I spoke again.*

*"You mean more than marrying the love of his life,
Lord? More than having kids?"*

*"Yes," came the kind answer. "I have more than
made up for these things, Steve."*

I understood in that moment what God was saying to me:
Josiah was experiencing things so inexpressible—right at that
very moment—that earth's best experiences could only pale in
comparison. The Father's words to my heart began to settle the
storm inside. At the very least, His promise put the shoreline
back in my sight. And looking back, I see now that His words
launched me on a journey toward the mysteries of Heaven. It
was one of those God-moments that allow you to place a stake
in the ground, where the revealed Word changes you in ways
that are difficult to fully articulate. Please don't mishear me, the

hurting still remained after my shower encounter, but God's answer to my pained complaint began the process of binding up a father's broken heart and bringing fresh hope to our family.

GOD OF THE LIVING

The word "living" means active, knowing, feeling, participating, communicating, and remembering. It means having life, being alive, not dead. It can also mean thriving, vigorous, and strong. Our God is a God of the living, not the dead. Jesus reminded His audience of who God is in Matthew 22:31, 32: "Have you not read what was spoken to you by God, saying, 'I am the God of Abraham, the God of Isaac, and the God of Jacob'? God is not the God of the dead, but of the living."

Jesus was speaking to the Sadducees, a group that accepted only the first five books of the Old Testament as Scripture, and they rejected a physical resurrection of believers, because they saw nothing in their Scriptures to support the doctrine. In this verse, Jesus quoted Exodus 3:6 and pointed out that when God spoke those words to Moses, Abraham, Isaac, and Jacob had been physically dead for many years. However, they were alive in Heaven with God. Jesus wanted us to know that life continues in Heaven.

Jesus was saying, "What about Abraham? Well, he is just

as much Abraham today as he ever was." Abraham, Isaac, and Jacob have been simply transferred from earth to another place. They are not dead; they are alive. This is true of our son, and it is true of your loved ones who are in Christ and waiting for you in Heaven. This is a glorious and hope-restoring truth!

We can also have hope that our family relationships will continue in Heaven. To illustrate His point that God is the God of the living, Jesus specifically mentioned family members—Abraham, Isaac, and Jacob. Isn't it wonderful that Jesus honored family relationships? He could have mentioned other people, but He chose a family. He was saying that relationship is beyond the grave. Relationship, family, and connection are not over—they don't stop. We have found that thinking any other way minimizes God and minimizes our trust to maximize everything He provides us on both sides of the veil.

After Lazarus passed away, Jesus told Martha in John 11:25, 26, "I am the resurrection and the life. He who believes in Me, though he may die, he shall live. And whoever lives and believes in Me shall never die." Since God is the God of the living, why do we talk about people in the past tense who have passed on to Heaven and refer to them as dead? They are alive, and they are forever an "is" in Christ. We must change our vocabulary. We have it backwards, and we need to change how we think and speak. Our words need to match biblical truth. We need to replace "dead" and "was" with "living" and "is." Why are we having such pity toward the saints in Heaven? They are the ones who have been swallowed up by life (2 Corinthians 5:4), and when they get swallowed up by life, guess what? They live!

In John 11:26 Jesus continued his conversation with Martha. He asked her, "Do you believe this?" Martha had just buried her brother four days earlier. Clearly, she was mourning big-time. Jesus brought the truth of the resurrection to her grieving mind, and then He put her on the spot and asked, "Do you believe this or not?"

In the midst of our grieving, we have the opportunity to think about the hope of the resurrection, and like Martha, we have to make a choice—a faith choice. Simply, the choice is this: do you believe? What's true on your best day must be true on your worst day. Jesus gives us that hope of resurrection, and you have a choice—to believe and feel His hope or to not believe and have no hope.

When you trust that believers never truly die, everything changes. It changes your focus, your vocabulary, your sorrow, and your mourning. It gives you hope to look at this conversation between Jesus and Martha and to think on these things, rather than on the negative things we're used to hearing. God is the God of the living. He is the God of Abraham, Isaac, and Jacob, and He is the God of all of us who have accepted Christ and who have loved ones with Him in Heaven. Since believers will never truly die, we'll be eternally present, not separated. This is a promise from God.

UNLIMITED POTENTIAL: OUR NEW BODIES

When we understand the power of God and the unlimited potential of Heaven, nothing should surprise us. He's prepared this special place and will give us heavenly abilities far beyond anything we could imagine here on earth. Just look at John 14:1–3 and how Jesus explained our heavenly home. He said, "Let not your heart be troubled; you believe in God, believe also in Me. In my Father's house are many mansions; if it were not so, I would have told you. I go to prepare a place for you. And if I go and prepare a place for you, I will come again and receive you to Myself; that where I am, there you may be also."

Here Jesus was talking about a special place that He is preparing. How awesome could that be? Jesus Himself is getting something very special together for all who believe. He said, "Don't be troubled—believe in Me. And oh, by the way, I'm taking it upon Myself to prepare a place for you. And, when you're ready, I'll be ready to receive you."

So what is He preparing? Is it an estate? Is it a house with an ocean view? Maybe, but it is also most definitely a new body. We don't read much in the Bible about the exact structures we might live in in Heaven, but God did give us a glimpse of what our celestial bodies will be like. We will get amazingly new spiritual bodies that are just like the resurrected body Jesus has. Matthew Henry wrote, "The happiness of heaven is spoken of as in a father's house. There are many mansions, for there are many sons to be brought to glory. Mansions are lasting dwellings. Christ will be the Finisher of that of which he is the Author or Beginner; if he has prepared the place for us, he will prepare us for it."[3]

Our new bodies will be "lasting dwellings" in which we'll have power that we cannot imagine. All of 1 Corinthians 15 deals with the issue of our heavenly bodies, and in verses 40–44 Paul wrote:

> *There are also celestial bodies and terrestrial bodies; but the glory of the celestial is one, and the glory of the terrestrial is another. There is one glory of the sun, another glory of the moon, and another glory of the stars; for one star differs from another star in glory.*
>
> *So also is the resurrection of the dead. The body is sown in corruption, it is raised in incorruption. It is*

sown in dishonor, it is raised in glory. It is sown in weakness, it is raised in power. It is sown a natural body, it is raised a spiritual body. There is a natural body, and there is a spiritual body.

Because of the Fall and the Curse that's on mankind, our current, earthly bodies are in a state of corruption, decay, dishonor, reproach, weakness, and frailty. However—praise God—our resurrected, heavenly bodies will be raised in immortality and incorruption. They will be characterized by glory and honor and power and supernatural abilities. This is so radically important for us to understand as we go through the grieving process: you will be raised to Heaven with this new and better body, and the believers who have gone before you already have theirs. They are raised in glory, living gloriously right now with God.

Our heavenly bodies will bear some resemblance to our earthly bodies, but they will be vastly different in terms of their abilities. Our new, resurrected body might look the same, but it will be infinitely beyond anything that we've experienced here on earth.

In 1 Corinthians 15:48, 49 Paul continued, "As was the man of dust [Adam], so also are those who are made of dust [our earthly bodies]; and as is the heavenly Man [Jesus], so also are those who are heavenly [believers with heavenly bodies]. And as we have borne the image of the man of dust [Adam], we shall also bear the image of the heavenly Man [Jesus]."

What was Paul saying? He said that just like we're in the same old dust/clay kind of flesh-and-bone body as Adam was, there's going to be a change. Just like we were connected with Adam, our resurrected bodies are going to be connected with Christ, the heavenly Man. We are going to have the exact same kind of body that Jesus Christ received when He was resurrected from the grave.

Now, that's a staggering thought. At least three different times,[4] Scripture tells us we'll have the exact same kind of body as Jesus, and guess what, beloved? The Creator of the universe didn't skimp on His own body. When He made it, when He thought it up, He wasn't thinking, *Well, I gotta limit it to this or that, or I probably won't be able to do that.* No way. God creates beauty and power.

When you think about Christ's resurrected body, with all of its unique abilities—including miraculously appearing (John 20:26), instantly disappearing (Luke 24:31), and flying (Acts 1:9)—it's pretty exciting to think we'll have the same kind of body and that our loved ones who are with Jesus have one right now.

Here's another story that illustrates our point. It's found in Luke 24:36–43:

> Now as they said these things, Jesus Himself stood in the midst of them, and said to them, "Peace to you." But they were terrified and frightened, and supposed they had seen a spirit. And He said to them, "Why are you troubled? And why do doubts arise in your hearts? Behold My hands and My feet, that it is I Myself. Handle Me and see, for a spirit does not have flesh and bones as you see I have."

> When He had said this, He showed them His hands and His feet. But while they still did not believe for joy, and marveled, He said to them, "Have you any food here?" So they gave Him a piece of a broiled fish and some honeycomb. And He took it and ate in their presence.

The major point of this appearance is the tangible nature of the body of the resurrected Lord. The risen Jesus has flesh and bones, and thus He is no vapor-like spirit/ghost. He can even eat a piece of broiled fish! Jesus allayed His followers' fears, dealt with their doubts, and made His bodily (not merely spiritual) presence unmistakable.

PRESENT WITH THE LORD

Not only are our Christian loved ones alive and enjoying a new, fabulous heavenly body, but they are also present with the Lord in Heaven. While vacuuming one day, the Lord unexpectedly interrupted me (Sarah). Out of the blue He said, "Josiah just lives in another country." With that I replied, "Whose builder and maker is God" (Hebrews 11:10, 16). You see, I knew exactly what God wanted to communicate: "Sarah, approach this as if Siah is only in another country . . . because that is the truth." Josiah is not afar off, and that truth set me free. Creator God went out of His way to open my eyes to the nearness of our son.

A week or so later after my conversation with the Lord, I felt compelled to look in *Strong's Concordance* for the full meaning of a scripture that had brought so much comfort in those initial days, 2 Corinthians 5:8. In that verse Paul wrote very authoritatively: "We are confident, yes, well pleased rather to be absent from the body and to be present with the Lord." It amazed me that the word *absent* means "to immigrate," and the word *present* means "to be in your home country." Siah truly has immigrated to his new home country. Because we fully believe that Josiah is alive and present with the Lord, the words "loss," "lost," and "death" aren't words we use around our house. We haven't lost anything, and nobody is dead. We know exactly where our son is, and he is very alive. We've learned to speak of him only in the present tense, because those who have been swallowed by life (2 Corinthians 5:4) haven't become a "was." In Christ, we are an eternal "is." What powerful truth in times of grief and sorrow—our loved ones are alive, and they are home with the Lord.

PICKLED

Everything we have shared in this chapter—that our Christian loved ones are fully alive in Heaven, present with the Lord, and enjoying a new heavenly body—has brought our family tremendous hope and strength in the midst of our grief. However, just because you believe something with all of your heart doesn't mean that Satan isn't going to try to put doubt in your mind or try to twist the truth of God's Word. I (Sarah) wish I could say that the Enemy of my soul took a break during the aftermath of Josiah's accident. But unfortunately, I cannot. Most moments, in the weeks that followed, I felt the Lord closer to me than my own breath. But there were other moments when Satan whispered into my ear, tormenting me with a very specific issue regarding my son. As a mother, the issue cut so painfully close to the bone that I chose to keep silent about it for a long time. I knew only the Lord could answer the deepest question of my heart. Also, I didn't want to burden my family, in case they were not struggling in the same way that

I was. The last thing I wanted to do was to add to the pain of my husband or my children.

The Enemy's specific torment surrounded our decision to have Josiah's physical body cremated after he underwent the organ donation process. Satan would taunt me, saying that because we had chosen cremation for our son, he would never be able to have a resurrected body (1 Corinthians 15). During those spiritual attacks, I encouraged myself in the Lord, remembering that Scripture definitively says that *whenever* the Enemy speaks he is lying, because he is the father of lies (John 8:44). I also knew that if God could breathe on the dust of the earth and create Adam and Eve, surely He could do the same with Josiah's physical ashes on the day of bodily resurrection. In addition to standing on the truth of God's Word, I began to ask the Lord to speak to this issue, knowing that He was the only One who could truly untangle the knot inside my mind and heart. For several weeks, without saying a word to anyone else, I continually asked my heavenly Father to speak to me regarding this tender issue of cremation, Josiah's physical body, and Satan's torment. And then one night, Josiah showed up in a dream. God's timing really spoke to me—it was during fall break, which was when Siah had told me he would be back for his first break from school.

In the dream, with a grin on his face, Josiah said two very odd words to me: "I'm pickled!" I knew immediately that this was an unusual statement, and it gave me a strong desire to understand the word "pickled" more fully. The Lord often speaks to me in riddles, so as is my custom, I grabbed my *Webster's Dictionary* and studied the word *pickled*. I found that when something is pickled, ultimately, it is preserved. The pickling process preserves the item. Understanding that pickled is synonymous with preserved, I began to search the Scriptures for the occurrences of the word *preserved*.

In Luke 17:33 Jesus said, "Whoever seeks to save his life will lose it, and whoever loses his life will preserve it." He was clearly saying that losing our life, surrendering it completely to Jesus, is actually preserving it. The Greek word for preserved is *zoogoneo*, and it means "to be engendered alive, rescued, and saved." Siah had surrendered his life to Jesus; therefore, Jesus has preserved Siah's life. Being reminded of that truth helped me big-time. Another Greek word used in several scriptures for preserved is *suntereo*. It means "to preserve, to keep close together." In Matthew 9:17 Jesus said, "Nor do they put new wine into old wineskins, or else the wineskins break, the wine is spilled, and the wineskins are ruined. But they put new wine into new wineskins, and both are preserved." Siah had surrendered his life to Jesus; therefore, Jesus has preserved Siah's life. That truth set me free.

Josiah, in Heaven, is preserved. He is still fully Josiah, and he is held closely together. He has a new wineskin, a new body, that is wonderfully and powerfully preserved in God's very presence. What a wonderful answer to my questioning mother's heart!

I found one more meaning for "pickled" that I want to throw out there for consideration. I find it curiously interesting that "pickled" can also mean to be drunk, to be intoxicated. This bears asking a question: are our loved ones in Heaven not only pickled as in preserved, but also pickled in the sense of being drunk, intoxicated, filled to the fullest with God's presence and power, supernatural gifts of love and joy, and more godly pleasure than we've ever dreamed of? That wouldn't surprise me a bit—in fact, it seems likely with all we know about Heaven. I couldn't help but remember that on the Day of Pentecost, when Jesus' followers were filled with the Holy Spirit, the onlookers said the disciples were "full of new wine" (Acts 2:13). Then Peter straightened them out by saying, "No, these men aren't drunk, they are recipients of the promise, power, and supernatural gifts of God mentioned in the Book of Joel." Here's a fun and fascinating thought: if being filled with God's Spirit, power, and gifts on earth was associated with being drunk, how much more pickled might we be in Heaven?! Psalm 16:11 says that in His presence is "fullness of joy" and at His right hand are "pleasures forevermore." Just a thought.

I love the many ways the Lord uses dreams. Dreams and visions have always been a way for God to talk to His people, and Peter reminds us that that hasn't changed (Acts 2:17). God used dreams to instruct Jesus' father to flee to Egypt and to tell him when to come back to Israel. He used a dream to warn Pharaoh of an impending famine. He used a dream to foretell the greatness of young Joseph's destiny. And He used a dream in my life to further unfold the greatness of Heaven, to reinforce the supernatural preservation of my son, and to firmly silence the Enemy's lying tongue.

If Satan is attacking one of God's promises in your own heart, ask Him to confirm the truth in your spirit by whatever means He deems best. It may be through a dream, or He may use some other method to deliver His message. Based on our experience, Steve and I firmly believe God answers questions that are too painful to even voice and that He loves to quiet the Enemy on our behalf. Yes, God is that good.

There are saints

in Heaven and saints

on earth who are

praying.

They are active

There shall be no more curse,
but the throne of God and of
the Lamb shall be in it, and His
servants shall serve Him.

~Revelation 22:3

I say, in Heaven our loved ones who have gone to be
with Christ see, hear, speak, sing, rejoice! Life is fuller,
richer, more glorious, more real with the saints in
Glory than with the saints on earth. [1]

~ Dr. John Rice

We know that our Christian loved ones are preserved and alive in Heaven, enjoying some pretty rockin' new bodies, and that they are present with the Lord. But that doesn't really tell us what they're doing in Heaven, does it? We do not believe that God went to all the trouble of saving us and giving us eternal life just to take us to be with Him in Heaven and then bore us to death for the rest of eternity. Might there be resting, might there be some leisurely harp playing? Sure! But there's also a lot of heart-pumping, meaningful activity in Heaven. Some people get nervous when we ascribe real living to eternal life, but if our concept of eternal life doesn't mean eternal living, then we're missing the point. That emphasis on eternal living affects how we live on both sides of the veil! So, as we started to unpack what the Bible tells us about Heaven, we wondered, *What are Siah and the multitude of others who are eternally with God doing right now?* The answers may very well surprise you.

THEY ARE PRAYING

The Book of Revelation is a great place to go for answers on Heaven. Revelation 5:8 says, "Now when He had taken the scroll, the four living creatures and the twenty-four elders fell down before the Lamb, each having a harp, and golden bowls full of incense, which are the prayers of the saints." This is a picture of the saints offering up their own prayers to Christ, prayers for all the redeemed.

We typically think of the praying saints as being the prayer warriors here on earth. Scripture doesn't make that distinction. There are saints in Heaven and saints on earth who are praying. We'll see this very clearly in our next two passages.

Revelation 6:9 says, "When He opened the fifth seal, I saw under the altar the souls of those who had been slain for the word of God and for the testimony which they held." These souls John saw were martyrs. Verse 10 continues, "And they cried with a loud voice, saying, 'How long, O Lord, holy and true, until You judge and avenge our blood on those who dwell on the earth?'" These saints who were martyred on earth cried out in prayer to God, asking Him to answer their heartfelt request.

Revelation 8:3 reminds us again about the prayers of the saints: "Then another angel, having a golden censer, came and stood at the altar. He was given much incense, that he should offer it with the prayers of all the saints upon the golden altar which was before the throne." Once again we see the faithful in Heaven actively praying. "All the saints" literally means "all the saints." Our loved ones, your loved ones, and every inhabitant of Heaven—all the saints!

These verses clearly tell us the saints are praying and crying out with a loud voice, which tells us this: right now in Heaven, there are people with emotions, feelings, and desires. The martyrs in Revelation 6:9, 10 cried—it literally means shrieked—out with a loud voice. They're more alive than we are. They cried out with a loud voice, and what did they say? "How long, O Lord, holy and true, until You judge and avenge those who have spilled our blood?" What does that tell us about them? It tells us they're emotional and that they have desires for God to intervene in the affairs of earth. It also tells us they know what's happening on earth and that they're interceding in Heaven right now. These martyred saints knew that the vengeance and justice hadn't taken place yet, and they petitioned God to make it happen.

These verses in Revelation also tell us that the saints in Heaven have a memory. It's not like they've gone to Heaven and now everything that happened on earth is just forgotten. They're not just floating around as some kind of oblivious spirit beings. No, they are very real. They are very alive. Their memory is filled with the things that happened on the earth. The martyrs knew their blood had been spilled; they knew they were martyrs. There is continuity between this life and the next, and our memories will remain intact.

Are our loved ones in Heaven able to occasionally see things that are happening on earth? Are our loved ones able to look down on us, see what's going on, and then say, "Hey, Jesus, could you touch my mom? Could you touch my friend? Lord, they're having a hard day and need some encouragement"? Do the saints intercede for people who are going through hard times? Yes—they know what is happening, as much as God allows, and they are praying for us! We know this might surprise you, but it's right there in Scripture. And we thought they were just playing harps . . . no way!

As we'll discuss more in the next chapter, the saints are aware of things that are going on in our lives. It's not all the time; they don't get to see everything. But every once in a while the Lord grants them permission to look on this earth, and based on what they see, they intercede on our behalf. The saints in Heaven are shouting their lungs out for God to intervene in the things of earth! Isn't that a wonderful connection to have with our loved ones who have gone before us? We need to recognize their participation in prayer.

God does things that are mind-blowing and beautiful and wonderful, and the fact that those who have gone to Heaven are alive and active and participating and doing things we don't give them credit for is because we imagine them in a minimized Heaven. Why do we minimize the activity of the saints in Heaven, when everything about Heaven is maximized? Everything about Heaven is bigger, it's grander, it's more alive—yet, in our humanity, we try to put a ceiling on it. Somehow we think the saints are doing *less* in the land of the *more*.

Our view of God radically affects how we view Heaven. If we see God as a stingy, reluctant withholder, then we'll see Heaven as sterile, boring, and predictable. If we see God as a loving, generous Father, then we'll see Heaven as the land of exclamation points—a limitless place full of surprise and wonder!

THEY ARE WORSHIPING AND REJOICING IN GOD'S PRESENCE

> *I'll praise my Maker with my breath;*
> *And when my voice is lost in death,*
> *Praise shall employ my nobler powers;*
> *My days of praise shall ne'er be past,*
> *While life and thought and being last,*
> *Or immortality endures.*[2]

As this old hymn states, the saints in Heaven are worshiping and rejoicing in God's presence. The Book of Revelation gives us many glimpses of the ongoing worship service that is happening right now in Heaven. The four living creatures, the twenty-four elders, the angels, and "every creature which is in heaven" (including departed saints) worship God with these words in Revelation 5:13: "Blessing and honor and glory and power be to Him who sits on the throne, and to the Lamb, forever and ever!" Check out another worship scene John witnessed in Heaven:

> *I looked, and behold, a great multitude which no*
> *one could number, of all nations, tribes, peoples,*
> *and tongues, standing before the throne and before*
> *the Lamb, clothed with white robes, with palm*
> *branches in their hands, and crying out with a loud*
> *voice ... saying: "Amen! Blessing and glory and*
> *wisdom, thanksgiving and honor and power and*
> *might, be to our God forever and ever. Amen."*[3]

Can you imagine worshiping God with every nation, tribe, people, and language? We were created to worship God, and just as it ought to be now on earth, our entire life in Heaven will be one big act of worship, only everything will be maximized beyond words compared to our best attempts at worship here on earth. It's hard to imagine how amazing it will be to look on the face of the One we love and adore. Our friends and family members in Heaven are worshiping Him right now—face-to-face!

In addition to worshiping God, the saints in Heaven are also rejoicing in God's presence. In Luke 15:10 Jesus said, "Likewise, I say to you, there is joy in the presence of the angels of God over one sinner who repents." This is one of the most misquoted verses in all of the Bible. The verse doesn't say that the angels are rejoicing. It says that there is joy *"in the presence of the angels"* (emphasis added). We've traditionally given that job over to the angels because surely it couldn't be the departed saints . . . because they just sit around and do nothing, right?

Wrong. We're sure that the angels do rejoice when someone comes to faith in Jesus Christ. We're sure that God rejoices when someone comes to faith in Jesus Christ. We know that about His character and nature. But Luke 15:10 specifically says there is joy in the presence of the angels of God, and we believe wholeheartedly that this joy includes the departed saints. These saints have been praying and hoping and praying and hoping that their loved ones on earth, whom they can see, would come to Christ. Then, when that person comes to Christ, they rejoice! The departed see, and they know when someone comes to Christ. We believe that with all our hearts.

THEY ARE ENLISTED IN GOD'S SERVICE

Along with praying, worshiping, and rejoicing, the saints in Heaven also have work to do. Revelation 7:15 says that the saints "are before the throne of God, and serve Him day and night in His temple." Revelation 22:3 says, "There shall be no more curse, but the throne of God and of the Lamb shall be in it, and His servants shall serve Him." Work was ordained by God before the Fall, so work itself was not part of the Curse (Genesis 2:15). We were created to have meaningful work, and whether our heavenly occupation will be related to our earthly occupation or the special gifts and interests God has hard-wired into each person's DNA, we know that working in service to the King in any capacity will be a joy.

Speaking of service, some, maybe all, saints are literally enlisted in God's service as members of the armies of Heaven. These warriors are described in Revelation 19:11, 14: "Now I saw heaven opened, and behold, a white horse. And He who sat on him was called Faithful and True, and in righteousness He judges and makes war. And the armies in heaven, clothed in fine linen, white and clean, followed Him on white horses." Clearly, from the description of their clean, white robes, these warriors are not warring angels, but warring saints. Their attire matches that of the saints in Revelation 7:9, 10, 13–17.

These warriors are enlisted right now, and Satan certainly recognizes this army. Revelation 19:19 says he will gather his forces to make war against this army of saints. Satan is prepared for an all-out war, so how could we possibly think that the Lord's army will be untrained and unprepared for this epic battle? The word *army* certainly implies activity, training, missions, etc., and it's hard to imagine Heaven as quiet or mundane when you consider the strength and training and passion that go into being an enlisted member of an active army. Along with their mighty Commander-in-Chief, the armies of Heaven will be victorious and will return to earth with Jesus at His Second Coming, to reign and rule with all the saints (1 Thessalonians 3:13; Jude 14, 15).

During his years on this earth, Josiah definitely had a warrior mindset. So much so that we even researched what it would take for him to become a Delta Force Operator. Knowing this about our son, we couldn't help but wonder what his job might be in God's heavenly army. As we'll share in the next two sections, the answer we received was astounding.

GONE FISHING: GOD'S ANSWER TO A GRIEVING MOTHER'S HEART

Only two weeks after Josiah went to Heaven, I (Sarah) made it a habit to talk to Josiah after dropping Destiny, our youngest, off at school. I would hold back my tears all the way to her school and then let them go the instant we said good-bye. I would then be in instant conversation with Jesus and Siah. I would stretch my hand out across the passenger side of the car and say,

> Siah, I want to know what you are doing. I need to be involved with your life even now, even in Heaven. I know that you are doing kingdom work, and I want to be involved in what you are doing. Father, I know that You know what is best for me to know, and so because of Your great mercy, I am asking You this question: "What is Josiah doing now?" I believe that, after nineteen years with my child, You wouldn't say, "No, Sarah, you may not know." That is not who I have known You to be all these twenty-five years. And so, I am asking.

I had no immediate answer to my bold request, but I have

learned to wait on the Lord, to trust Him in every quiet place, to pour out my grief on Him, and to allow Him to be near to the brokenhearted (Psalm 34:18). I learned to excavate His Word in ways I had never done before. His Word became literal life to my bones. I ached to be close to Jesus, knowing He was "a Man of sorrows and acquainted with grief" (Isaiah 53:3). During this time, I settled in my heart that if, for some reason, it was not beneficial for me to know about Josiah's activity in Heaven, I would surrender to that. However, the "ask" still burned within me, and I truly believed God would answer the cry of my mother's heart in His way, in His time.

On a Sunday I will never, ever forget, a friend named Sammy approached us after our eleven o'clock service. Sammy said he needed to speak with us urgently. About a year and a half ago, Sammy and his wife, Zainib, served as live-in interpreters for an Iraqi girl who lived with us while she received medical care in Nashville. During this time, he became a close family friend, and he developed a special bond with Josiah. We knew from Sammy's face that he had something major to share. Steve and I went to the altar and sat down, facing an obviously nervous Sammy. There he told us that he had had a dream about Josiah. He explained this experience in the best language that he could—he said it was a dream, yet it was more than a dream and very real. So with tears in his eyes and trembling hands, Sammy began to unfold the dream:

> Steve and Sarah, I was riding in a car with you and Destiny, and we were heading for the lake. The lake was close, but it took a long time to get there. When we arrived, we began walking on the beach. Then I asked Steve, "Is this the sea or lake? I cannot see to the other side. Why are we here?"
>
> Steve answered with a smile, "Well, someone said it is a good place to be."
>
> Then Sarah said, "Destiny and I are going to explore the other side of the beach." With this, Sarah and Destiny left the dream.
>
> Steve was facing the sea, and I was behind him. Steve then said to me, "Sammy, we need to be leaving soon." In the dream, I realized that the sun was going to set soon, and we needed to climb a hill to get back to the car so we could leave before the sunset.
>
> At this point Josiah came walking up from Steve's right, and he was facing the sea. Josiah was carrying a fishing pole. Josiah and Steve said a casual hello, as if they had not been apart. Then Josiah said, "Dad, I don't want to leave. I want to stay and fish."
>
> Steve answered, "Josiah, you don't know how to fish."

Josiah answered, "Yeah, I know. But I met this Guy, and He is teaching me how." Josiah then pointed the opposite way, and we turned to look. There was a Man in a robe who lifted a staff and nodded to confirm that He was the Man they were speaking about.

"Okay, Josiah, you can stay," Steve answered.

Josiah replied, "Yeah, Dad—there are a lot of hungry people and a lot of fishing that needs to be done."

Steve asked, "Where are all the people?"

Josiah answered, "Dad, you know what I mean." Then Steve and Josiah said their good-byes. Josiah happily picked up his pole and bounded back down to the beach. He was visibly happy.

The dream continued. I became upset with Steve because I believed that he had just missed his opportunity to bring Josiah home. Then we started walking up the hill to the car. I began to pull on Steve's shirt and asked him, "Where are we anyhow, and what is going on?"

I turned for one last look at the lake and saw that there were several people fishing. They were visiting and laughing as they cast their lines. Where Steve and I stood, the sun had set. I could see that it was brilliant and bright where Josiah fished back down *at the sea. Steve never answered my question. He didn't even take a second look at the lake, but he did turn to me and give me a knowing smile.*

We almost couldn't believe what Sammy was sharing with us. But he wasn't quite finished. He told us that the minute he awoke from the dream, he woke up Zainib and asked her to run and get him a glass of water, because he felt he had just been climbing and was extremely thirsty. He felt physically exhausted.

I (Sarah) looked at Sammy and asked him, "Sammy, do you know what Jesus says about making us fishers of men?" He looked at us and replied, "I don't know anything the Bible says about fishing. All I know is that the boy [Dallas] had the dream about Josiah leaving his hospital room with God, and I remember thinking, *What happens now in Josiah's life?* I am a Muslim [our church has a significant ministry reaching out to new refugees in the area, many of whom are Muslim], but I believe God gave me this dream because you are my family. I wondered where Josiah is and what he is doing now, and I thought, *Steve and Sarah must wonder, too.*"

At this point, Sammy looked directly in my eyes and said, "I want you to know, Sarah—Josiah has a job, and Josiah fishes."

Later on, we continued to unfold the Scriptures to Sammy,

explaining to him that the sea represents humanity, that God Himself is the Light, and that Christians who have gone to be in Heaven are still active, as God wills it, in kingdom work (as evidenced by the fishing). We also shared that the kingdom of Heaven is like his description of traveling to the lake: it is nearby (within all believers; Luke 17:21) but far away (it will not be fully realized until Jesus sets up His kingdom on the New Earth; Revelation 21). The image of Jesus teaching Josiah how to fish and how to feed hungry people aligns perfectly with something Jesus told His disciples He came to do: make them fishers of men (Matthew 4:19). Although we don't fully understand the details of how or in what way, we believe that Josiah is participating in the "catching" of unbelievers for Jesus Christ. This belief is evidenced by the fact that hundreds have come to Christ because of Josiah's life and legacy. In fact, in one recent altar call, a young man told us, "Your son has caught me."

After two weeks of waiting for an answer, Creator God answered my "ask."

Now, you may be wondering while reading this account of Sammy's dream why in the world God would choose to use a Muslim man who has zero biblical knowledge to deliver a message about Heaven and about what Josiah is doing right now. If you're scratching your head, consider that this is not the first time God has used unbelievers to deliver an important message. And more importantly, this is not the first time God has used a dream to draw unbelievers to Himself. When God wanted to announce the birth of His Son, He did not just appear to the local shepherds outside Bethlehem. No, He hung a bright star in the vast sky and planted the idea in the hearts of three pagan wise men to make a life-changing journey. They followed the star because they believed it would lead them to the King of the Jews. And later, God again used these men by warning them in a dream not to return to Herod and disclose Jesus' location (Matthew 2:1–12). Consider Pilate's wife, who received a message from God in a dream that her husband should not participate in Jesus' trial and crucifixion (Matthew 27:17–20).

God can choose to use anyone to accomplish His will—He is neither limited in the way He ministers to His children nor restricted in the way He draws unbelievers to Himself. We praise Him for His unusual, yet biblical methods!

MISSIONS FROM HEAVEN

Multiple times over the last fifteen years, we have read a very compelling book entitled *My Dream of Heaven* by Rebecca Ruter Springer. In this fascinating little book, Springer relates her vision of what Heaven is like and details the kinds of activities she witnessed there after she was transported to Heaven during an extended life-threatening illness. She was inspired to write the book after recovering from her near-death experience, and we found Billy Graham's endorsement to ring very true: "*My Dream of Heaven* . . . captures Biblical truths with emotional impressions." One of the most emotional impressions the book left on us was Springer's idea that saints in Heaven go on "invisible missions" to earth. Let us share two such examples. In the book, one of Springer's friends in Heaven relates her experience of visiting with her mother, who was still alive on earth, to comfort her:

> I am with her often, but her great, and I fear unreconciled, sorrow, keeps me from being the comfort to her I long to be. If only she could spend one hour with me here [in Heaven], could know God's wisdom and love as we know it, how the cloud would lift from her life! How she would see that the two lives, after all, are but one.[4]

Springer's brother Frank was also in Heaven, and she tells in the book that part of his heavenly ministry was to make trips to earth for the Master. Speaking to the frequency of such missions, she said of him, "'He stands very near to the

Master,' and *I [know] how often He was sent upon missions to the world below*"⁵ (emphasis added.) Do saints in Heaven go on invisible missions to earth? Is it out of the realm of possibility? Consider this dream that Josiah's ninth-grade English teacher had:

> I, too, believe in the power of dreams. In my dream [Josiah's] spirit was near the water in Thailand, but not on the beach. It was an area with a great deal of plant life. It was the twilight of the evening; the sun had just set, and it was very calm, warm, and tranquil.
>
> Josiah's name had been carved into the top of a reed-like plant—picture a broomstick cut in half—that was sticking in the mud on the edge of the water. His name was carved in a circular pattern where it had been cut. I was not privy to the specifics or the reason for the carving, but I remember hearing Josiah's spirit saying that he was in Thailand because that is where he was needed. My dream ended with that.
>
> Josiah touched many lives. I hope that his spirit is still touching lives somewhere in the world.

A GREAT APPEARING

So, do saints in Heaven go on invisible missions to earth? Before you decide too quickly, consider the account of the

Transfiguration in Matthew 17:1–13. Verses 1–3 set up this famous story: "Now after six days Jesus took Peter, James, and John his brother, led them up on a high mountain by themselves; and He was transfigured before them. His face shone like the sun, and His clothes became as white as the light. And behold, Moses and Elijah appeared to them, talking with Him."

Now, could you imagine being Peter, James, and John? Jesus said, "Hey, come on up the mountain with Me, guys," and as they were sitting there waiting for another one of Jesus' great sermons, all of a sudden, something miraculous happened. We don't know what kind of sound effects went down, but they were likely pretty awesome as Jesus was transfigured before their eyes. His clothes were as white as snow, and—wow!—His face shone, but it didn't stop there.

Two other people, Moses and Elijah, showed up after Jesus was suddenly transfigured. Isn't it amazing that two guys who had been in Heaven for hundreds of years were chosen by God to show up on earth? Moses had been in Heaven fifteen hundred years and Elijah six hundred, and they made this appearance to not only Jesus but the disciples as well. Moses and Elijah were heavenly inhabitants whom God sent to earth to participate in His redemptive purpose for mankind—and they talked with Jesus!

What did they talk to Him about? Matthew's Gospel doesn't tell us, but Luke's Gospel does. Luke 9:31 tells us that they were talking to Jesus about His upcoming death in Jerusalem. This clearly shows that people in Heaven know what's happening here on earth. People in Heaven knew what Jesus' ministry was and what He was about to do, and Moses and Elijah talked to Jesus about God's redemptive plan. They were participating in it as eyewitnesses and as communicators of it.

Once again we see that our God is the God of the living and not the God of the dead. God does things that are mind-blowing and beautiful and wonderful, but many people can't get their minds around the idea of departed saints being alive and active and aware. The saints right now are doing things that we don't give them credit for because we imagine them resting in peace instead of participating in God's kingdom work. What we do know is, those in Heaven right now are alive and active. They have emotions and desires. They intercede and participate in God's redemptive plan. They have memories of life on earth, and they know things that happen here. They surround us. They worship. They serve. They learn and live right now.

They are aware and present

*Your father Abraham rejoiced to see My day,
and he saw it and was glad.*

~ John 8:56

---

*Something quite unexpected has happened. . . .
Suddenly at the very moment when, so far, I
mourned H. least, I remembered her best. Indeed
it was something (almost) better than memory; an
instantaneous, unanswerable impression. To say it
was like a meeting would be going too far. Yet there
was that in it which tempts one to use those words.
It was as if the lifting of the sorrow removed a
barrier. . . . And the remarkable thing is that since
I stopped bothering about [forgetting my wife],
she seems to meet me everywhere. Meet is far too
strong a word. I don't mean anything remotely like
an apparition or a voice. I don't mean even any
strikingly emotional experience at any particular
moment. Rather, a sort of unobtrusive but massive
sense that she is, just as much as ever, a fact to be
taken into account.*[1]

~ C. S. Lewis

Jesus said in John 8:56 that Abraham rejoiced to see
His day and that when he saw it he was glad. Jesus was

clearly saying that Abraham could see Jesus' earthly ministry from Heaven and that it brought him joy. Many commentators miss Abraham's heavenly perspective and try to explain away this saying by making it a metaphorical statement rather than the simple truth that Abraham was aware of Jesus' manifestation to the world.

Hospice chaplain and psychotherapist Dianne Arcangel has heard hundreds of stories over the years from people who are in the midst of a painful grieving experience. Many of her clients believe they have had tangible experiences with their loved ones, such as dreams or symbols or sounds, and some of the experiences have been confirmed by more than one person. To help her clients make sense of these experiences and explore their veracity, she set out on a five-year study called "The Afterlife Encounter Survey." The result was a book, *Afterlife Encounters: Ordinary People, Extraordinary Experiences*. We don't agree with many things in the book, but the things that line up with Scripture are very interesting. In the book Arcangel reports that "64% of the bereaved who responded had an afterlife experience following the death of a loved one. Furthermore, an astonishing 98% of those said the encounter had brought much comfort and helped them cope with their grief, even many years later."[2]

Now, let's say right up front we're not talking about channeling, séances, or mediums trying to contact the dead. That's not what we're advocating and not what we're saying. Deuteronomy 18:10 forbids seeking those types of encounters.

What we are saying is that the Bible makes it clear that our loved ones in Heaven are alive, active, and aware—and we need to have heart and understand their vitality and nearness. We need to understand that God has the power to temporarily lift the veil between Heaven and earth at any time according to His good pleasure.

SAMUEL AND SAUL

Let's look at 1 Samuel 28:15–19:

> *Now Samuel said to Saul, "Why have you disturbed me by bringing me up?"*
>
> *And Saul answered, "I am deeply distressed; for the Philistines make war against me, and God has departed from me and does not answer me anymore, neither by prophets nor by dreams. Therefore I have called you, that you may reveal to me what I should do."*
>
> *Then Samuel said: "So why do you ask me, seeing the Lord has departed from you and has become your enemy? And the Lord has done for Himself as He spoke by me. For the Lord has torn the kingdom*

out of your hand and given it to your neighbor,
David. Because you did not obey the voice of the
Lord nor execute His fierce wrath upon Amalek,
therefore the Lord has done this thing to you this
day. Moreover the Lord will also deliver Israel with
you into the hand of the Philistines. And tomorrow
you and your sons will be with me. The Lord will
also deliver the army of Israel into the hand of the
Philistines."

Though Samuel had departed from the earth, he was still keenly aware of Saul's past and present disobedience. More than that, he knew about God's future judgment of Saul, his sons, and the nation of Israel. Let's be clear, 1 Samuel 28:12 says the medium saw Samuel. This wasn't some kind of demonic spirit. It was Samuel coming from Heaven. Why did God allow this? We don't know, and that's not our purpose. What we do know is, Samuel showed up. Again, we're not saying the saints know and see everything. It's just clear from Scripture that sometimes they know what's happening here on earth.

IT'S A TRANSITION, NOT THE END

James Garlow and Keith Wall share the following story in their book, *Heaven and the Afterlife*. They write of a woman named Evelyn whose father passed at eighty-nine from a heart attack. Evelyn missed him terribly, feeling depressed and empty, and then something happened that brought her great joy:

It was the first time my mother and siblings had all come to my house after Daddy died. We were missing him but not talking about it much.

One of Daddy's favorite things was to gather around the piano together and sing our way through a couple of hymnals. This was somewhat stressful for me, since I don't play the piano very well, and he had a knack for picking the most difficult hymns. But that was easily overcome by his lovely tenor voice, and the way we bonded through the music. Eventually, other people would drift in and join us.

I'm not sure how it happened without him there to get us started, but that day we all wound up around the piano. It was as if singing his favorite hymns was a safe way to let our feelings out.

After a while I slipped away from the group for a moment (my sister was playing the piano) and went into the living room. I stopped in my tracks when I saw Daddy sitting there in his old rocking chair. He looked younger and healthier than he was before he died. He had a glow about him that's hard to describe. The look on his face was one of deep satisfaction, as though he was enjoying the music as much as ever, with no sense of regret that he wasn't still with us. He said, "It's so good that you are all singing."

All I could manage was, "Daddy!" He smiled, and I knew he was happy and well wherever he was now. Then, suddenly, he was gone. But the room was filled with deep peace and love that I have trouble expressing. Although I missed him, I can't say that I grieved for him after that. I knew he was still, for lack of a better word, alive and that we'd be together soon.[3]

Garlow and Wall go on to say that this experience filled Evelyn "with new hope that *death is not an end but merely a transition to a new state of life*. Until then she'd struggled with the fear that her daddy was lost forever and that with him had gone the love they shared. Within seconds that fear was dispelled and her healing began in earnest" (emphasis added).[4]

Unfortunately, this lovely woman's response to her father going to Heaven, prior to her meeting with him, represents so many in the church. Many believers honestly struggle with viewing a loved one's passing as "merely a transition to a new state of life," as Garlow and Wall put it. But we don't need to struggle—Scripture tells us there is great continuity between this life and the next and that our departed loved ones are alive, active, and aware in Heaven.

A SPECIAL VISIT

Several people in our family and inner circle of friends have experienced similar meetings with Josiah as Evelyn had with her father. We want to share one in particular that our Executive Pastor, Jim Sterling, experienced. Our church, Grace Chapel, sets aside every other Wednesday evening for prayer and worship services. This particular night was a worship service, and our friend Rita Springer was serving as a guest worship leader. Jim and his wife were in the back of the sanctuary. Jim recalls:

> Rita began playing the song, "It's Gonna Be Worth It." The song really touched me and took me to a deeper place with the Lord. There were many, many times in the hospital when we were at Josiah's bed praying, "God, this better be worth it." So hearing this song took me back to that place. As I was listening, I was praying, and I asked God one more time, "Lord, is it worth it?"

> The next thing I knew, Josiah came into the sanctuary. It wasn't like he just appeared there. It was a sense of him coming into the aisle, and he got down on one knee and bent to speak into my ear. He said, "Way worth it, Mr. Jim." Then, as quickly as he came, he left. It wasn't that he disappeared; rather, it was a sense of him leaving the sanctuary.

It was as Josiah as Josiah could be. He was dressed in a white T-shirt and white knee-length shorts, and his hair was white, like when he was a young boy. He had a sense of speed about him, not that he was hurried, but as if life here on earth was much slower than in Heaven—it's a different place, a different plane.

I stood up and went over to my wife and told her, "Josiah was just here."

Pastor Jim and Josiah have been friends for a long time. Josiah's special name for him is "Mr. Jim." Few people knew that. This visit proves that our loved ones in Heaven are spiritually active and that they care—they are aware of times that we need special encouragement. Josiah saw his friend, tired, questioning, and drained, and God granted Josiah permission to make an appearance to encourage and reassure him.

Jim was comforted by Josiah's visit, and it serves as proof that our son is not dead and gone, but merely moved to a different place to do other things for God. It shows he is happy there, and it demonstrates his continued presence in not only our lives but in the lives of his friends as well.

While rejoicing about the story, we told Rita Springer about Jim's experience, and she let us know about a special prayer request she made before worship began that night. She simply asked God, "Father, could Siah come worship with us tonight?" God answered her prayer. Josiah was near to the moment and gave Jim encouragement and hope. Yes, the residents of Heaven are personally present, they are aware, and they are near!

SPONTANEOUS

Our meetings with Josiah have been very much like the ones C. S. Lewis described in the quote at the beginning of this chapter. Lewis said that as he began to allow God to heal his broken heart, as the sorrow began to lift, he was then able to experience these supernatural visitations from his wife. It's important to note that these special encounters are spontaneous, not sought after. They occur when we are not grasping too intensely and when we are not striving to conjure something up in our own strength or imagination. As we said earlier, we're not talking about mediums or séances. God specifically warned the Israelites in Deuteronomy 18:10–12,

> *There shall not be found among you anyone who*
> *makes his son or his daughter pass through the fire,*
> *or one who practices witchcraft, or a soothsayer, or*
> *one who interprets omens, or a sorcerer, or one who*
> *conjures spells, or a medium, or a spiritist, or one*
> *who calls up the dead. For all who do these things*

*are an abomination to the L*ORD, *and because of*
*these abominations the L*ORD *your God drives them*
out from before you.

Do you remember the passage we talked about in an earlier chapter, Luke 24:36–43, in which Jesus appeared to the disciples after His resurrection? It's important to note that this visit was spontaneous. The disciples didn't seek it out. There was no go-between to make it happen. Jesus just showed up! And just like Evelyn's daddy, Jesus' appearance removed fear and replaced it with peace.

The apostle Paul wrote in Galatians 5:20, 21 that those who practice sorcery and witchcraft "will not inherit the kingdom of God." It's the spontaneity—like Evelyn's story or Josiah's visit to Pastor Jim or Moses', Elijah's, and Jesus' visit to the disciples—that makes the difference from condemned by God to orchestrated by God.

Garlow and Wall summarize it well: "What can a medium, speaking for a dead person, possibly tell you that you can't hear in Scripture and prayer? With God there is no potential for fraud, deception, contamination, or disaster."[5] To the grieving, these appearances by our loved ones need not be scary or too good to be true. They simply communicate the reality that our Christian loved ones are alive, active, and aware. If

God allows supernatural visitations in your life, thank Him for this precious gift!

CODY'S GOD NOD

From day one, we have communicated to our three kids on earth that Josiah is still a vital part of our family and, as God allows, still aware of things that go on in our home. We want all of us to continue to have relationship with Siah right up until the day that we are face-to-face in Heaven with him. We're not saying that Siah is appointed to be with us every moment, but when he is, we know that he delights in the fact that we share our hearts with him. Proving again that Siah is aware of things going on here on earth, we received the following God Nod:

> I (Sarah) remember a day a few months ago when our sixteen-year-old son, Cody, asked Steve if he could go mudding in the Jeep. The Jeep was previously Josiah's, and it was always said that when Siah went to college, the Jeep would then become Cody's. The bog that Cody went to mud in is located within a short distance from our house, so I watched as he ventured off for the first time, four-wheel drive activated and ready to conquer. As I watched Cody drive away, I could hear Siah saying in my spirit, "Cody was always better at those things than me. I am proud of him."

Hawk Heart

We can't really explain it, but it was so quick and so random, I just knew it was Siah. The Lord once again knew what would touch Cody's heart—an encouraging word from his older brother. Later that day as Cody and I visited in Josiah's room, I shared what I had experienced as I watched him track through the mud. It brought a tear to his eye and joy to his heart.

We have explained to the kids that Siah cannot read our minds; only the Lord can do that. But it must make Siah so happy to see that we get it. We know he can see us, hear us, and even be involved, not only in our lives but also in the lives of his friends. We are continually hearing of Siah coming to friends in dreams (and we've shared a few in this book). The dreams are incredibly profound and always prove God's Word, point to the glory of God, and compel us to get closer to Jesus. Be on the lookout for God Nods in your own life.

Connected

So we, being many, are one body in Christ,
and individually members of one another.

~ Romans 12:5

> We may be sure that all the saints and heroes of God
> cluster around the banisters of Heaven and gaze
> with the deepest concern upon us who are left here
> to run our race! And the force of the argument is
> that, since the grandstand of Glory is filled with so
> many eager observers, we should lay aside every sin
> and the besetting sin of unbelief and look to Jesus
> to complete (finish) our faith, and we should run our
> race with patience.[1]
>
> ~ Dr. John Rice

UNIVERSAL COMPANIONS

Many people, after hearing about the dreams and visits we've had, ask, "How close are the saints? Is there an ongoing relationship?" In our quest to better understand Heaven and the things of Heaven, we turned to the Book of Hebrews:

> Therefore we also, since we are surrounded by so
> great a cloud of witnesses, let us lay aside every

> *weight, and the sin which so easily ensnares us, and*
> *let us run with endurance the race that is before*
> *us. . . . But you have come to Mount Zion and to the*
> *city of the living God, the heavenly Jerusalem, to*
> *an innumerable company of angels, to the general*
> *assembly and church of the firstborn who are*
> *registered in heaven, to God the Judge of all, to the*
> *spirits of just men made perfect.*[2]

The writer of the Book of Hebrews went to great lengths
to describe how close our loved ones are: we are *surrounded* by
a great cloud of heavenly inhabitants! Hebrews 12:1 is right
after Hebrews 11, the hall of faith chapter, which describes
many heroes of the faith who departed and went to Heaven.
Here's a paraphrase of what the writer says in 12:1: "Therefore—because of what I just got done telling you, because of
all these great people who are in Heaven now—understand
this: we are surrounded by a great cloud of witnesses." We're
surrounded. It literally means that the saints are lying down
all around us. There are so many it's innumerable. They are
spectators, and they are all around us.

Hebrews 12:22, 23 says that we have come to an innumerable company of angels, the departed saints, and God. This
general assembly isn't just the angelic hosts, but also a general
assembly of the church, which means this: our loved ones in

Heaven are our universal companions. This general assembly of the saints is the great cloud of witnesses. They are the onlookers.

This fact should bring tremendous comfort and hope. It's something we need to know and cling to when the Enemy tries to convince us of other things. Our Christian loved ones in Heaven are not "dead" or "lost"; they are surrounding us and serving God. If one of the reasons the saints in Heaven are surrounding us on earth is to encourage us to lay aside the weight of sin and run our race with endurance (Hebrews 12:1), consider which one motivates you more: the thought of an Old Testament prophet in your corner or the thought of your precious loved one who knows you intimately and loves you completely. That's a no-brainer as far as we're concerned! We mean no disrespect to the prophets, but the idea of Siah being able to observe the choices we make here on earth is way more motivating as we seek to live for God moment-by-moment. The cloud of witnesses is personal, and we believe it is part of their work in the spiritual realm to cheer on their loved ones still on earth and encourage them to throw off the weight of sin and run the race of life as unto Jesus, "the author and finisher of our faith" (v. 2).

Here's an amazing fact: God, Heaven, and its inhabitants

are the focal point of satanic blasphemy (Revelation 13:6). I (Steve) believe satanic attack has so infiltrated the church that there are even some believers today who want to minimize Heaven's unlimited glory. Why try to minimize anything about Heaven or its inhabitants when everything about Heaven is maximized? If the Enemy can't get us to *not* believe in Heaven at all, his next best desire is for us to believe in a minimized, predictable, boring Heaven. And we refuse!

WE ARE ONE BODY

The fact that the veil is thin between our loved ones and us shouldn't shock us. Let's read what Paul said in Ephesians 3:14, 15: "For this reason I bow my knees to the Father of our Lord Jesus Christ, from whom the whole family in heaven and earth is named." Paul was saying that we are *one family*, with *one name* in *Heaven* **and** *earth*. We are one body, not two. There isn't one body on earth and another in Heaven. We're one body.

The phrase "is named" from Ephesians 3 literally means "is derived." The whole Christian family—including those saints now in Heaven with Jesus as well as those of us still living on earth—"derives" its spiritual life from God. He's the leader, we're the followers, and we're together as one body without regard to where we are, in Heaven or on earth. One of many scriptures that speak about the "one body,"[3] Romans 12:5, says, "So we, being many, are *one body in Christ,* and individually members of one another" (emphasis added).

The one body spoken of by Paul in Romans 12:5 is truly THE body of Christ, and it's here on earth as well as in Heaven. Our family has been supported by the body here on earth and by the body in Heaven. We can imagine that the saints who are in Heaven have been praying for us since day one of this trial and that they continue to pray for us as we grieve. They are joining the prayers of our friends here on earth to give us comfort, peace, and hope. Oh, the beauty of the body of Christ!

You have the same body in your corner. There is one family, one name, one body, and we're all eternally connected on both sides of the veil.

CONNECTED NOW AND FOREVER

Josiah and his friend Jimmy were planning to attend the University of Tennessee together. Shortly after the accident, Jimmy had a dream about Josiah. As they were talking in the dream, Jimmy felt uncomfortable because he didn't want to mention that Josiah had gone to Heaven. So his conversation was nervous, afraid that his best friend and soon-to-be college roommate would leave if he mentioned anything to him about his passing. Finally, Josiah broke the uncomfortable conversation and told Jimmy, "I'm fine, Jimmy. I know I'm in Heaven. I just want to visit. I came to make sure you are okay."

Jimmy's dream is a great example of how we are surrounded and our loved ones are connected to us. They know, they care about what we're going through, and there's a nearness that's not easy to explain but wondrous in reality.

We are *one* body, connected here on earth, connected in Heaven, and connected between Heaven and earth. Our loved ones may show up in dreams or visits or other ways (who can limit God's imagination?), but the fact is that we're connected. Our loved ones are not "up there" and we are "down here." There is a thin veil, and we're connected to them, forever, in Christ.

HEATHER'S GOD NOD

Heather, our oldest daughter, had a request of the Lord. She was so saddened that she and Siah seldom expressed their strong love for each other during their days together on earth. She wanted so desperately to have another chance to tell him how much she loves him. She shares her God Nod here in her own words:

> After Siah went to Heaven, naturally my mind began
> to wonder what I should have done differently while
> he was physically on earth with me. We had our
> occasional arguments or irritations with each other,
> but it was never anything substantial, so I didn't have
> regrets over any of that. The only thing I wished I had
> done more was to tell him how much I love him. We
> always knew how much we loved each other, but
> we didn't say it out loud nearly enough. Ironically,
> the most that we had ever said "I love you" to each
> other was over the last two months before he went
> to Heaven, because I was in China on a missions trip.
> Every time we would e-mail or instant message, we
> would **always** finish our conversation by saying "I
> love you!!" Even at that time I was so grateful for those
> loving exchanges, but I did not realize how much
> more they would mean to me just a few weeks later.
>
> Even though we had been more open and frequent
> about saying "I love you," I still felt like I hadn't done
> it enough. But the Lord has given me a few chances
> to make up for lost time. I have had three or four
> dreams with Siah in them since the accident. None
> of them have been super deep, but they have had
> a big influence on me nonetheless. Every time Siah
> shows up in a dream, it is my first reaction to tell
> him how much I love him. As soon as I see him, I just
> have this sense of urgency to run up, grab him, and

just tell him that I love him as many times as I can in our time together. He always says it back, but during one dream in particular he responded by saying to me, "I love you forever." This might sound like a cliché response, but when I told my mom about the dream and she looked up the actual definition of the word "forever," we discovered it means "eternal" and "perpetual." Siah was telling me that he loves me now and will continue to love me for our eternity together.

The Lord knew the desires of my heart and gave me the opportunity to live it out. Now I feel more at ease not only knowing that Siah knows how much I love him, but also knowing that he will love me forever.

Our connection with our friends and family in Heaven is current, ongoing, and it is forever. Our perpetual love for one another will never stop!

God nods

*If you then, being evil,
know how to give good gifts to your children,
how much more will your Father
who is in heaven give good things
to those who ask Him!*

~ *Matthew 7:11*

Earth has no sorrow that Heaven cannot heal.[1]
~ *Dr. John Rice*

In the very beginning of the book we introduced God Nods, and we've sprinkled some of those Nods throughout the book. These kinds of special, supernatural moments radically contribute to the healing process. They come spontaneously and when we least expect them. We are compelled to record these supernatural visitations for ourselves and for those who may take courage and believe in deeper, more supernatural experiences because of these stories. We'd encourage you to recognize when God shows up in the midst of your sorrow.

SWEET SOMETHINGS

The Lord has been so good to us. From the get-go, our prayer for our kids, their friends, and for us as parents has been:

> *Lord, we do not want to be comforted by men, by something that is not eternal and true. We do not want to find solace in a word that isn't Yours or an experience that is not from You. Only the truth, Lord, is what we ask for. You say that Your grace is sufficient, so You are enough.*

We have learned to trust all the more in His voice. He is continually speaking, yet many so seldom hear His voice. He is continually showing Himself, but many close their eyes and count it all as coincidence. So, here are some sweet somethings, a few more precious God Nods, that the Father has allowed in our own family. These experiences have been a rope of hope, tethering our hearts to Heaven and reminding us that we are eternally connected with Josiah.

DESTINY'S GOD NOD

As we said our last good-byes to Siah in the hospital, our daughter Destiny kissed him several times on the cheek. They have always had a sweet relationship, as do the other kids with

Siah, just different. One day upon arriving home from a brief trip, Destiny with excitement began to tell us the most incredible story. "Siah kissed me twice on the cheek," she said. Knowing Destiny would *never* make up such a thing, nor would her imagination take her there (she is a pretty literal girl), we immediately agreed that it really was Josiah. She began to unfold the story of how she had been sleeping in the early morning and felt someone lie down beside her and kiss her twice on the cheek. In that moment she thought it was Sarah and figured we had arrived home much earlier than expected. But then in a heartbeat she knew that it was Siah. She said, "I just knew it was him. I didn't need to open my eyes—I just knew, because in the hospital I kissed him the very same way." Remember, God knows what our hearts long for, and He answers our cries. This encounter with Siah brought Destiny so much joy.

THE WHITE CRANE: GIFTS FROM THE LAND OF THE LIVING

On the third day after Josiah went to Heaven, I (Steve) awakened again in an emotional and spiritual daze. I said a very specific prayer, fumbled around for my robe, slipped on some flip-flops, and headed off down our steep driveway toward the pond that sits right in front of our house. As I approached the small body of water, something very unusual caught my eye immediately. However, before I can tell you that story—and I promise I will—I need to tell you another.

As a young minister pastoring my first church, Calvary Chapel Pomona Valley, I had the opportunity to befriend some of God's most beloved and unique kids. Early on, a handful of hard-core motorcycle riders began attending our fellowship. One of these men, Darrell, had been what's known in the biking world as a "One Percenter"—a term used to identify those who led the most dangerous, crime-riddled lives in the biker gangs. However, like millions throughout history, God had other plans for Darrell. Darrell met Jesus, and Jesus healed his broken heart and made him a new creation in Christ. On the outside he still looked like someone you might be afraid to run into on a deserted street, but inside he was as soft as a newborn baby. Darrell and his wife, Val, immediately got busy ministering to others who were involved in his former life and even helped to form a motorcycle group called "Soldiers for Jesus" that would ride together and then have Bible study and fellowship. I had the honor of teaching some of these men in my church as well as in their Bible study from time to time.

Several years into his journey with Jesus, Darrell suffered a massive heart attack. He was rushed to the hospital and was informed by the doctors that, because of the abuse he had put his body through while in the gang life, his heart was irreparably damaged. "A limp, wet washrag" was the phrase they used to describe the failing organ in Darrell's chest. The doctors could do nothing, and they knew it. Darrell knew it, too. He immediately called his friends and loved ones to the hospital and began saying good-bye to each of them, knowing his time on this side of Heaven was short. During that short time in the hospital, Val asked Darrell to send her a sign to let her know he was all right and "home" in Heaven.

Val had always wanted a baby possum. You read that correctly . . . not a dog or a parakeet or even a pet turtle, but a baby possum. Who wants to raise a possum? And even if one did, where would one find it? Darrell and Val lived in Garden Grove, CA, a veritable cement city. There were no places for wild life (or wild critters) to even live. Possums, squirrels, raccoons, and the like were unheard of in Garden Grove. But that didn't squelch Val"s desire.

So, fast-forward to a few days after Darrell's memorial service. Val was at home with her two daughters when one of the girls made a startling discovery in the hallway. There, right there, in the middle of the hallway were two live baby possums. Two! These possums were Val's answer to her heartfelt hospital request: "Can you please send me a sign to let me know you are all right?"

This story lived in infamy in our household for years. Everyone in our family and in our close circle of friends knew about the sign of the possum. It was one of those true stories that make you curiously scratch your head at the wonder and mystery of God. I never, though, knew that one day I would need my own possum miracle. That day had arrived.

Now, let's go back to the day in question: I mentioned previously that as I rose I prayed a very specific prayer. The prayer was a simple and desperate one: "Lord, I need my possum." I was begging God for a sign, a sign as out of the ordinary as God's baby possums were to Val that my Josiah was all right. His safety was something I "knew" with my spiritual eyes, but I was asking God to give me something I could behold with my physical eyes. So, having prayed that prayer, I rose. Flip-flops, robe, and all, I headed down the driveway toward the pond. And there it was.

It was stark and solitary. It was stately and clearly out of its ordinary place. In the five and a half years that we have lived in our house, one has never been at our pond before. It took my breath away. It was a huge, white crane. Unusual on any day, but incredibly unusual during a season like this, I was immediately intrigued and crept closer, expecting at any minute to see the tall, statuesque bird take flight. But it never did. I went closer and closer, and the bird remained. It stayed and stayed and stayed.

Have you ever seen a white crane up close? With a wingspan of nearly seven feet and an elegant, long neck, they are something to behold. Interestingly, they are endangered in most areas. They're uncommon. The visitor at the pond definitely got my attention. I remember thinking, *I wonder what this could mean.* For that long moment, something bigger than grief gripped my heart, and even though I didn't know exactly how, I suspected that the Lord was answering my request for a sign about Josiah.

I tucked my avian encounter away and continued through the day. For two days, I pondered these things in my heart (Luke 2:19), saying nothing to anyone. A few mornings later, I was walking with my two brothers, Mike and Patrick. Something about moving physically seemed to keep the pain at bay a bit. I did a lot of walking in those days. Rounding the old barn behind our church and walking slowly toward the main building, I saw Jim O'Brien, our Children's Pastor, standing there. To this day I don't know what possessed me to ask Jim the next question: "Jim, does a white crane mean anything to you?"

He looked stunned for a moment and then answered slowly, "White Crane was the type of martial arts I was teaching Josiah."

I knew that Siah was training with Jim in Kung Fu, but not White Crane.

I've walked with the Lord for twenty-five years, and I know when He is hanging a bell on something. I suspected this was one of those times. At Jim's request, Sarah and I got together with him a couple days later, because he said he had something important to share with us.

Jim handed us a plaque with our son's name—Josiah David Berger, Champion—written on it. I knew it was official looking, but it didn't quite connect until Jim began to explain. Siah had called Jim the night before his accident, and their sweet conversation that night was a kiss from God to Jim when looking back. They visited for some forty-five minutes, and it was then that Josiah mentioned his desire of wanting to earn a black belt in White Crane. After Josiah went to Heaven, before I had even seen the white crane at our pond, Jim had felt urged to go through the official steps to make Josiah an honorary White Crane black belt. A first-degree black belt himself, Jim knew firsthand the seriousness and difficulty of becoming a black belt. People typically train for many, many years to achieve such a goal. Josiah had only trained for about a year and a half. In spite of this, Jim located a martial arts training facility and explained that one of his students (Josiah) had passed away and was worthy of receiving the black belt, even though he did not have all the required training. Since being a black belt ultimately means being a defender of the defenseless, Jim knew Josiah fit the bill, even more perfectly than most, as he so selflessly demonstrated by donating of his "earthy" body to help seventy-seven people in need. Josiah had literally defended life.

At the dojo, Master Stephens took Jim through the ceremony to honor Josiah as a fallen black belt hero. Interestingly, during the moment of silence honoring Josiah, Jim's gaze fell upon something extremely unusual in the martial arts world. In the middle of the table, in a place of extreme prominence, sat a lone Bible. This only served to further confirm God's hand in pursuing this honor for Josiah.

Even though Jim does not personally adhere to the spiritual beliefs of martial arts (nor do we), he found the history of the white crane to be interesting. In ancient martial arts culture, it was believed that when a warrior fell, a white crane was sent to the family as a sign of assurance. And in the book *Symbols of the Christian Faith*, it states that cranes are symbolic of resurrection—not a bad gift for a dad whose son just went to Heaven![2]

All I know is that my loving, intimate heavenly Father gave us all a sign and a gift that our Josiah was home.

I got my possum.

God wants us to fully

understand His power,

His beauty, His majesty,

and His will.

Rejoicing in the legacy

Therefore we do not lose heart. Even though our outward man is perishing, yet the inward man is being renewed day by day. For our light affliction, which is but for a moment, is working for us a far more exceeding and eternal weight of glory, while we do not look at the things which are seen, but at the things which are not seen. For the things which are seen are temporary, but the things which are not seen are eternal.

~ 2 Corinthians 4:16–18

It's not our job to raise doctors, dentists, schoolteachers, homemakers, mechanics, entertainers, and so forth. It is our job to raise children who give their lives to God and commit their lives in service to Him.[1]

~ Billy Graham

When we began to write this book, we wanted it to minister to two groups of people: those who are grieving and those who need a renewed, biblical vision of Heaven. If you are reading this in the midst of grieving, we know it's not easy, and we know there may be days of tears, anger, and sadness. However, our trust needs to be in Jesus, and our hope needs to be in Heaven. With that foundation, we want to share some things in this chapter that may help answer the question of how to define a new normal and continue living here on earth while we wait to be reunited in Heaven with our loved ones. We all need to find a way to grieve with hope and rejoice in our loved one's legacy.

GRIEVING WITH HOPE

From the beginning of our journey, we've had a burden to help other believers deal biblically with the issue of Heaven. We realized that we needed to really dig into the Word on this subject and shed some light on what the Bible says about eternity and how to grieve with hope. Teaching others what God has revealed to us about Heaven is one of the ways we honor Josiah, and it also helps us to find purpose in this journey.

We pray that the picture we have painted in this book of Heaven and of what the saints are doing right now will allow all of us to grieve with hope, not despair. Once you understand God's truth, once you go after the Lord in the midst of your sorrow, then you can grieve with hope. Once you understand more about where our loved ones are, what they are doing, how alive they are, and the fact that they are present and near, then you can have peace and grieve with hope.

Grieving with hope also includes understanding and feeling God's sweetness. You don't father or mother a child for nineteen years and then hear God say, "Oh, now you can't talk to him. You no longer have a relationship with him until you see him face-to-face in Heaven." You aren't a husband or a wife or an aunt or a grandparent and suddenly God's character changes from sweetness to stinginess in not allowing you to feel that special closeness. We still talk to Josiah, and it's going to be so great when we're together again.

Earlier we wrote about what Jesus said in John 11:26. He said that believers "shall never die," and then He asked, "Do you believe this?" Remember, when you believe that, everything changes. It is impossible for death to prevail in His presence! Everyone who clings to Him and is united with Him in faith will live with Him eternally. Christians will pass through an incident called physical death, but they cannot die eternally because they have put their trust in the One who is life. That's our hope and our reality.

Jesus directed His question in John 11:26 ("Do you believe?") to Martha after her brother, Lazarus, passed away. It appears she didn't fully grasp the total meaning of what Jesus had said, but she accepted Him. She said, "I believe that You are the Christ, the Son of God, who is to come into the world" (v. 27). This means that Jesus was standing with her in the presence of death, knowing with her the pain and terror, but offering life that can turn sorrow and separation into joy and wonder. This is also our hope and our reality. Do we grieve? Yes we do, and in the beginning it was a moment-by-moment struggle.

Early in this journey the Lord gave me (Sarah) this verse: "If you loved Me, you would rejoice because I said, 'I am going to the Father'" (John 14:28). If we unconditionally love our family and friends who have gone to Heaven, we by God's grace should one day arrive at a place where we can actually be happy for them. They are alive. It is far better. And they are with Jesus. This allows us to grieve with hope.

OPEN DOOR POLICY

We have always had open, communicative relationships with each of our children. So, it was important for all of us from the beginning of this journey to be able to share our tears, fears, dreams, blessings, and doubts openly with one another. We're an "all-for-one-and-one-for-all" kind of family, and nothing about that has changed since Josiah went to Heaven. There are times when Josiah is so crazy-close. We so want to ask God,

"Please, just peel back the veil a bit and let us see Josiah with our physical eyes. We know he's here. Just for a second, Lord." But we know it would not be beneficial. We cling to the hope that Josiah is a member of the one body of Christ and that he may very well have knowledge of what we're going through. We know he has something important to do for God, and we know he's in a new body. We know, too, that we'll be joining him when it's the right time—God's time.

But until we're reunited in Heaven, we want, as do the kids, to keep our relationship with Josiah alive and current and relevant. One of the ways we've symbolized this connectedness in a physical sense is to leave Josiah's room as Josiah's room and to always leave his bedroom door open. The "open door policy" we've always had with the kids has come to mean something even more since Siah left. We don't believe he still resides in his old room, but to us, it feels natural to keep his room as is since he is still a vital and active part of our family. It's our way of honoring Josiah's legacy and symbolizing the place he holds forever in our hearts and in our family.

MANAGING YOUR MEMORIES AND GUARDING YOUR HEART

Memories are like roads. We can choose which roads to travel and which ones to avoid. Philippians 4:8, 9 says:

> *Finally, brethren, whatever things are true,*
> *whatever things are noble, whatever things are*
> *just, whatever things are pure, whatever things are*
> *lovely, whatever things are of good report, if there is*
> *any virtue and if there is anything praiseworthy—*
> *meditate on these things. The things which you*
> *learned and received and heard and saw in me,*
> *these do, and the God of peace will be with you.*

Paul is saying, "Meditate on these things." He is urging us to meditate on the truth of God and to plant it deep in our hearts and minds. Allow Jesus Christ to renew your mind each day, and ask the Holy Spirit to direct you to thoughts that are true, noble, just, pure, lovely, good, virtuous, and praiseworthy. Take every thought captive (2 Corinthians 10:4, 5), and if it is dark, lonely, bitter, or hurtful, throw it out! Those thoughts are of no use to you.

We know it's not easy, but we can also tell you that when we do this—when we meditate on the things Paul writes about in these verses, when we listen to the Comforter and refuse to go places in our hearts that are off-limits—there is healing.

We need to manage our memories and guard our heart (Proverbs 4:23) and let the Holy Spirit steer us down the right roads. We can't be looking back at who Josiah was. We have to live in the now. We need to choose spiritual roads, not emotional ones. Doing so helps us to have hope and helps us to give hope to others. Doing so will help you, too. Living in the now helps us understand that Josiah's still alive, and it helps us see that what he's accomplished through people's lives carries with it a powerful legacy.

Living in the now and managing our memories is not about living in denial. It is about realizing what we need to think about. There may be times when the Holy Spirit tells you, "Hey, this road isn't going to be good for you." Zero in on what the Holy Spirit is telling you, and don't allow yourself to get lost in memories that are not healthy for you to focus on because you think you're supposed to grieve a certain way. There may be a time in the future when He encourages you to take that road, or He may never release you in that direction. It boils down to trusting the Holy Spirit. He's our Comforter, He's our Helper, and He's the ultimate GPS, telling us what road to travel and helping us focus on what is truly hopeful and helpful. If we travel roads on which the Holy Spirit is not leading us, we forfeit comfort and add to our sorrow. We would encourage you to only go where He leads and to stay focused on His truth about Heaven and your loved one who is there.

There may be times when you, like Jesus, might say, "My

God, My God, why have You forsaken Me?" (Matthew 27:46).
Jesus knew the Father hadn't forsaken Him. But He felt it,
and He said it. When you are grieving, you may feel that way,
too. This feeling, however, needs to be the exception, not the
rule. By walking in the Spirit, focusing on the truth of God's
Word, and concentrating on the reality of your loved one's
life and his or her presence in Heaven and the active work he
or she is doing, you will stay where you need to stay—that's
the road you want to travel. None of this ever completely
takes away the missing, that's for sure, but it's the right road
to take and the right road on which to stay.

Take the right road, beloved—don't let the Enemy of this
world destroy the heavenly picture that the Word gives us
and the hope we have for today and the future.

DIVING DEEPER

Several well-meaning friends gave us books on grief in the
days and weeks after Josiah left for Heaven. The only ones
that ever brought comfort were those about Heaven. In others
there seemed to be this common thread of relating grief to a
tidal wave that picks you up, thrashes you around, and finally
leaves you alive on the beach. I (Sarah) understand this anal-
ogy oh so well and have felt at times worn out on that beach.

But the Lord has given me a different picture to focus on when I feel the pull of a mighty wave heading my direction.

As a child growing up in Southern California, I was taught to dive under waves. I learned early on that you can't stand—you need to go under or you will be toppled. In Laguna Beach there is a specific type of sea grass called eelgrass, and as a wave approached, I would dive under the waves and hold on to that grass. I could feel the wave at the surface and the force wanting to take me with it. Just as I learned to do in the ocean waves, the Lord encouraged me to do the same to withstand the waves of grief. His words to me were, "Dive deeper and hold on."

When I feel a wave of grief coming, I usually drop to my knees and ask the Lord through tears, "Take me deeper, Lord. Show me everything I need to know in this journey. I cannot bear that anything be wasted." We cry together and somehow I know that I have been with God and at times, even Siah. In my fellowship with Creator God, I am renewed and gain what moments before I may have lacked in my spirit—eternal perspective.

CELEBRATING THE LEGACY

After Josiah passed, we found a letter he wrote to himself

during a summer break three years ago. It describes a break-through he had with the Lord during a prayer session that he said was the best of his life. He wrote that he just wanted to go back to high school and influence people. He wanted to love people and show them his deep appreciation for them. God answered his prayer when he cried out to Him, and God is still answering that prayer. God was faithful to the cry of Josiah's heart.

Josiah's pre-accident decision to become an organ donor immediately saved five lives. We learned that seventy-seven people ultimately benefited from his decision to donate his organs. We know that the man who received his heart is fifty-five with five children and five grandchildren. He's alive and doing very well today. We know the people who received his kidneys, and in the words of the donor society, "Josiah saved their lives." His work on earth continues.

A tremendous amount of spiritual work happened in the hospital. God radically touched many of Josiah's friends. We witnessed them trusting God and crying out to Him, all while loving and serving our family and one another. And that spiritual work hasn't stopped.

As of this writing we are planning on taking twenty-three of Josiah's friends to the Dominican Republic to put the finishing touches on four orphans' homes for young boys. By the way, those homes will collectively be called "Josiah's House Village." Josiah has a heart for children, particularly orphans and underprivileged kids, and we know that this project is bringing him tremendous joy as he looks down from Heaven. Talk about a legacy!

Your loved ones will have a legacy as well. Rich legacies aren't just for pastors of large churches and their kids. This is not about an elite club—every Christian has a legacy to be honored and cherished. Let us share another parent's story of legacy. Marilyn Heavilin is a woman with a love for the Word and a God-given ability to express what she has learned from the Bible in practical terms. Marilyn is the author of the popular book *Roses in December* and is an inspiration to all with her positive attitude and zest for life. Three of Marilyn's children are in Heaven. In 1964 Marilyn's son Jimmy went to Heaven as a result of crib death when he was seven weeks old. Twin sons, Nathan and Ethan, were born a year later on Christmas Day. Ten days after birth, Ethan went to Heaven due to pneumonia. And in 1983 Ethan's twin brother, Nathan, was killed by a drunk driver. Nathan was seventeen.

Nathan left a tremendous legacy. Marilyn is an active member of MADD and other grief counseling ministries. She's written a number of books and spoken worldwide to grief-stricken parents and others whose loved ones have passed. Her love for all three of her boys and her determination to help others is positive proof of how a tragic event can be turned into a significant legacy.

Marilyn had a choice to make. She could be consumed, or she could contribute. One of the greatest ways to help in your grieving is to serve others. Where might you get involved to serve and begin to build a legacy for your loved one who is now in Heaven? The cancer society? The mission field? A homeless shelter? A scholarship fund? You fill in the blank, but just know there's definitely something you can do to contribute to your loved one's legacy. Pray and ask God for His direction and His perfect timing. Don't give up—press on. Marilyn says, "My prayer was simply, 'Don't let it be wasted.' Forty-six years later, God is still using my boys' story. Praise God!"

Josiah, Marilyn's boys, and the multitude of others who have passed to Heaven have left their legacies for us. It's difficult to see at times, it's difficult to think about, but God loves you and your loved one so much that He's going to give you both a continuing and lasting legacy. Our loved ones are in that mighty cloud of witnesses, and they are cheering us on and seeing their legacy in changed lives, mended hearts, and redeemed souls.

GOD COMFORTS SO WE CAN COMFORT OTHERS

Second Corinthians 1:2–7 says:

> *Grace to you and peace from God our Father and the Lord Jesus Christ. Blessed be the God and Father of our Lord Jesus Christ, the Father of mercies and God of all comfort, who comforts us in all our tribulation, that we may be able to comfort those who are in any trouble, with the comfort with which we ourselves are comforted by God. For as the sufferings of Christ abound in us, so our consolation also abounds through Christ. Now if we are afflicted, it is for your consolation and salvation, which is effective for enduring the same sufferings which we also suffer. Or if we are comforted, it is for your consolation and salvation. And our hope for you is steadfast, because we know that as you are partakers of the sufferings, so also you will partake of the consolation.*

As we discussed in the chapter on brokenheartedness, God is the God of all comfort. He comforts us so we can comfort others with the same comfort He has given to us. Some people don't know where to go when they are hurting. When we know where to go, then we can give it away to other people and tell them where to get their own supply. God enables us to help heal others who are brokenhearted. His Spirit empowers us to do kingdom work.

Our successful suffering, brokenness, and healing let others know that they can endure their own brokenness through the comfort of Jesus Christ. Jesus needs to be alive in the hearts of all of us who are broken Christians. This world needs to see our faithfulness, and when they see it, they'll go, "You've given me hope. I can make it."

Jesus came to heal the brokenhearted, and He's the solution to your pain. Get to know Him, and draw near to Him. If you trust Him and come to understand the peace that surpasses all understanding, you will make it through this terrible life storm. You'll make it, not by the skin of your teeth, but by the strength of His Spirit. Then you'll be able to touch other people. This will turn your pain, your tragedy, inside out for the glory of God. What was once your misery can become your ministry. You can choose to praise God and minister to others. It's an honor and a privilege of the highest order. We must make a difference for Jesus Christ. Serving Him is the greatest and most lasting legacy we can leave in our loved one's honor.

We want to leave you with this passage from 1 Thessalonians 4:13–18:

> But I do not want you to be ignorant, brethren,
> concerning those who have fallen asleep, lest
> you sorrow as others who have no hope. For if we

believe that Jesus died and rose again, even so God will bring with Him those who sleep in Jesus. For this we say to you by the word of the Lord, that we who are alive and remain until the coming of the Lord will by no means precede those who are asleep. For the Lord Himself will descend from heaven with a shout, with the voice of an archangel, and with the trumpet of God. And the dead in Christ will rise first. Then we who are alive and remain shall be caught up together with them in the clouds to meet the Lord in the air. And thus we shall always be with the Lord. **Therefore comfort one another with these words** *(emphasis added).*

Our departed loved ones are alive in Heaven and coming back in the clouds with Jesus someday. If we're still here on that glorious day, we will be reunited with them instantly. Isn't God good? He lets us know that we aren't going to have to wait one second more than necessary to see our loved ones—He's bringing them back with Him! Comfort one another with these words.

EPILOGUE

We've shared a lot in this book. We hope it's helped you. We hope you better understand Heaven and the glorious, eternal condition of your Christian loved one(s). Of all we've told you, we strongly encourage you to remember two things:

God is Good.
His Word is Truth.

We could not be taking this journey without a foundation solidly poured. These two truths are the indestructible cement of our foundation. We believe them wholeheartedly, and these two truths are what continue to keep us focused in the right direction.

We also encourage you to go deeper. Dig into God's Word and discover what He has for you and specifically for your situation. Going deeper is much like taking a deep scuba dive. You have to stop along the way to decompress. The deeper you go, the more stops you need. We must settle early in the dive that God is good, and then proceed down into the depths of His truth. Divers who don't stop and decompress get very sick, and they lose the beauty and excitement of the dive. Take your time, go deep, and enjoy the revealed beauty. We know God wants to reveal wonderful, comforting truth to you. We know He'll speak to you in many different supernatural ways. Know that. Believe that. Have an ear to hear what the Holy Spirit is saying to you. Don't miss God's mighty, miraculous works due to unbelief (Matthew 13:58).

As this journey continues to unfold, we are building relationships with people who are looking for hope and are fascinated with Heaven. Visit us at www.haveheart.net. Please feel free to meet us there.

God Bless You,

Steve and Sarah Berger

HOW TO GET TO HEAVEN

It's not as complicated as you might think.

Jesus' first sermon is found in Mark 1:15. He said, "Repent, and believe in the gospel." Number one, you need to repent. It means to change your direction, to change your mind, to stop running *from* God and start running *to* God. God wants you to make a U-turn, and it's called repentance.

Second, you need to believe in the gospel. Believing isn't just mental or intellectual agreement. Biblically speaking, believing means trusting, clinging to, and wholeheartedly depending upon. You need to believe in the gospel with your heart, not just your head.

The gospel is summed up in John 3:16: "For God so loved the world that He gave His only begotten Son, that whoever believes in Him should not perish but have everlasting life." God loved you so much He sent Jesus to take the penalty of your sins and die in your place so you could live in Heaven forever with Him. You have to cling to that truth by faith.

John 1:12 says, "But as many as received Him, to them He gave the right to become children of God, to those who believe in His name." After you have repented and believed, you need to personally receive Jesus as your Lord and Savior.

Repenting, believing, and receiving can be done by a simple, yet eternally profound, prayer. It might sound something like this:

> *Heavenly Father, I repent. I turn to You now. I realize I can't get to Heaven on my own. I believe Jesus Christ took the penalty of my sin and died on the Cross in my place so I could know You, love You, and spend eternity with You in Heaven. I believe Jesus rose from the dead, and I receive Him now as my Lord and Savior. Thank You for accepting me into Your eternal family. Amen.*

If you have prayed that prayer from your heart, you have the assurance of what the Bible promises: you are now a new creation in Christ, old things have passed away, and all things have become new (2 Corinthians 5:17). Now, read God's Word and obey what you read.

Heaven is rejoicing!

ENDNOTES

INTRODUCTION
[1] Rebecca Ruter Springer, *My Dream of Heaven* (Tulsa, OK: Harrison House, 2002), ix.
[2] 2 Corinthians 4:16–18.

SO READY TO BE OUTTA HERE!
[1] Dr. John R. Rice, *Bible Facts About Heaven: Sweet Home of Departed Saints* (Murfreesboro, TN: Sword of the Lord Publishing, 1940), 29-30.

THE CELEBRATION
[1] Chris Tomlin, "I Will Rise," *Hello Love*. Compact Disc. Sparrow Records/sixstepsrecords, 2008. Used by permission.
[2] The entire service can be viewed by going to: http://gracechapel.net/ or http://haveheart.net/.

TURNING YOUR MOURNING INTO DANCING
[1] Steven Curtis Chapman, "Beauty Will Rise," *Beauty Will Rise,* Used by permission.
Compact Disc. Sparrow Records, 2009.
[2] Matthew 7:24–27.
[3] John 5:2–9.

HEAVEN REVEALED
[1] George MacDonald, *Sir Gibbie* (London: Hurst and Blackett, 1880), 191.
[2] Richard Leonard and JoNancy Linn Sundberg, comp., *A Glimpse of Heaven: Through the Eyes of Heaven* (New York: Harrison House, 2007), 103.
[3] This is an edited and anonymous version of an e-mail we received. It represents so many people who have questions.
[4] Hazel Felleman, *Poems That Live Forever* (New York: Doubleday, 1965).
[5] R. C. Sproul, *Surprised by Suffering* (Wheaton, IL: Tyndale, 1988), 135-138.
[6] Bruce and Lory Lockerbie, *Take Heart* (Grand Rapids: Fleming H. Revell, a division of Baker, 1990).

THEY ARE ALIVE
[1] "Dwight L. Moody quotes," ThinkExist, http://thinkexist.com/quotes/dwight_l._moody/.
[2] Henry Morris, PhD, "Alive Into Heaven," Institute for Creation Research, http://www.icr.org.
[3] Matthew Henry, *Matthew Henry's Concise Commentary on the Whole Bible*, Bible Gateway, http://www.biblegateway.com/resources/commentaries/Matthew-Henry/John/Christ-Comforts-His-Disciples.
[4] 1 Corinthians 15:48, 49; Philippians 3:20, 21; 1 John 3:2.

THEY ARE ACTIVE
[1] *Bible Facts About Heaven*, 19.
[2] Isaac Watts, "Psalm 146" [I'll Praise My Maker], *The Psalms of David* (Boston: Lincoln & Edmands, 1813). Original publication in England, 1719.
[3] Revelation 7:9, 10, 12.
[4] *My Dream of Heaven*, 75.
[5] Ibid., 120.

THEY ARE AWARE AND PRESENT
[1] C. S. Lewis, *A Grief Observed* (New York: HarperCollins, 1961), 44-45.
[2] Dianne Arcangel, *Afterlife Encounters: Ordinary People, Extraordinary Experiences* (Charlottesville, VA: Hampton Roads, 2005), 277-300.
[3] James L. Garlow and Keith Wall, *Heaven and the Afterlife* (Minneapolis: Bethany House Publishers, 2009), 71-72.
[4] Ibid., 72-73.
[5] *Heaven and the Afterlife*, 91.

CONNECTED
[1] *Bible Facts About Heaven*, 26.
[2] Hebrews 12:1, 22, 23.
[3] No less than seven times is "one body" mentioned in the New Testament.

"GOD NODS'"
[1] *Bible Facts About Heaven*, x.

[2] Alca William Steffler, *Symbols of the Christian Faith* (Grand Rapids, MI: Wm. B. Eerdmans Publishing Co., 2002), 57.

REJOICING IN THE LEGACY

[1] Billy Graham, *Living a Legacy* (Nashville: Thomas Nelson Publishers, 2007), 6.